GOLD TRADING 101

The Beginner's Guide to Unlocking the Potential of Precious Metals

Usiere Uko

Copyright © 2024 Usiere Uko

All Rrghts reserved.

No part of this publication may be reproduced, distributed, or transmitted in any form or by any means, including photocopying, recording, or other electronic or mechanical methods, without the prior written permission of the publisher, except in the case of brief quotations embodied in critical reviews and certain other noncommercial uses permitted by copyright law.
This publication is designed to provide accurate and authoritative information in regard to the subject matter covered. It is sold with the understanding that the publisher is not engaged in rendering legal, accounting, or other professional services. If legal advice or other expert assistance is required, the services of a competent professional should be sought.
The author and publisher shall not be liable for any loss of profit or any other commercial damages, including but not limited to special, incidental, consequential, or other damages.

ISBN-13: 979-8-327-77810-8

FIRST EDITION

CONTENTS

Title Page
Copyright
INTRODUCTION
PART 1: INTRODUCTION — 1
Chapter 1: Welcome to Gold Trading — 2
Chapter 2: The History and Allure of Precious Metals — 6
Chapter 3: What This Book Will Teach You — 11
PART 2: THE BASICS OF GOLD TRADING — 15
Chapter 4: How the Gold Market Works — 16
Chapter 5: Key Terms and Concepts in Gold Trading — 21
Chapter 6: Major Gold Trading Platforms and Markets — 25
PART 3: ANALYZING THE GOLD MARKET — 31
CHAPTER 7: Factors Influencing Gold Prices — 32
CHAPTER 8: Economic Indicators and Their Impact on Gold — 36
CHAPTER 9: Technical Analysis — 40
CHAPTER 10: Fundamental Analysis — 50
CHAPTER 11: Combining Technical and Fundamental Analysis — 54
PART 4: GETTING STARTED WITH GOLD TRADING — 57
CHAPTER 12: Setting Up Your Trading Account — 58
CHAPTER 13: Choosing a Broker — 63

CHAPTER 14: Trading Fees and Commissions	68
PART 5: DEVELOPING A TRADING STRATEGY	73
CHAPTER 15: Short-Term vs. Long-Term Trading Strategies	74
CHAPTER 16: Risk Management and Diversification	79
CHAPTER 17: Setting Goals and Limits	85
PART 6: TOOLS AND RESOURCES FOR GOLD TRADERS	90
CHAPTER 18: Essential Trading Tools and Software	91
CHAPTER 19: Reliable Sources for Market News and Analysis	96
CHAPTER 20: Educational Resources for Ongoing Learning	101
PART 7: PRACTICAL TRADING TIPS AND TECHNIQUES	105
CHAPTER 21: Reading Gold Price Charts	106
CHAPTER 22: Identifying Trading Signals and Trends	113
CHAPTER 23: Common Mistakes and How to Avoid Them	122
PART 8: ADVANCED GOLD TRADING STRATEGIES	126
CHAPTER 24: Options and Futures Contracts	127
CHAPTER 25: Hedging and Arbitrage Techniques	133
PART 9: LEGAL AND TAX CONSIDERATIONS	137
CHAPTER 26: Tax Implications of Gold Trading	138
CHAPTER 27: Record-Keeping Best Practices	140
PART 10: BUILDING AND MANAGING YOUR PORTFOLIO	142
CHAPTER 28: Portfolio Diversification Strategies	143
CHAPTER 29: Investing in Gold and Gold Assets	146
CHAPTER 30: Balancing Gold with Other Investments	161
CHAPTER 31: Periodic Review and Rebalancing	163
PART 10: THE FUTURE OF GOLD TRADING	165
CHAPTER 32: Emerging Trends in the Gold Market	166

CHAPTER 33: Technological Innovations and Their Impact	169
PART 11: FINAL THOUGHTS	172
CHAPTER 34: Final Tips for Successful Gold Trading	173
CHAPTER 35: Encouragement for Your Trading Journey	176
Glossary of Gold Trading Terms	179
Recommended Reading and Resources	185
Sample Trading Plan Templates	189
About The Author	193
Books In This Series	195
Books By This Author	197

INTRODUCTION

THE BEGINNER'S GUIDE TO UNLOCKING THE POTENTIAL OF PRECIOUS METALS

Welcome to "Gold Trading 101: The Beginner's Guide to Unlocking the Potential of Precious Metals." This book is your gateway to understanding and mastering the fundamentals of gold trading. Whether you are new to the world of investments or looking to diversify your portfolio, this guide will provide you with the essential knowledge and tools needed to navigate the dynamic and often complex gold market.

Basic Trading Strategies: Learn simple yet effective trading strategies tailored for beginners. We'll cover essential concepts such as leverage, margin, and risk management to help you start trading with confidence.

Regulatory and Tax Considerations: Understand the legal and tax implications of gold trading to ensure compliance and optimize your investment returns. We'll guide you through the necessary steps to navigate these important aspects.

Practical Tips and Resources: Benefit from practical tips and resources that will support you on your trading journey. From selecting the right trading platforms to staying updated with market news, we've got you covered.

By the end of this book, you will have a solid foundation in gold trading, equipped with the knowledge to start investing in precious metals effectively.

Whether your goal is to safeguard your wealth, achieve financial growth, or simply diversify your investment portfolio, "Gold Trading 101" is your essential guide to unlocking the potential of precious metals.

PART 1: INTRODUCTION

CHAPTER 1: WELCOME TO GOLD TRADING

YOUR GATEWAY TO THE WORLD OF PRECIOUS METALS INVESTMENT

Welcome to the exciting world of gold trading! Whether you're looking to diversify your investment portfolio or seeking new opportunities in the financial markets, gold trading offers a unique and potentially rewarding avenue. Gold has been cherished for centuries, not only for its beauty and use in jewelry but also for its enduring value as a form of currency and investment. Gold is also referred to as God's money, used through the ages as a store of value.

In this book, we will guide you through the fundamentals of trading gold online, helping you unlock the potential of this precious metal even when you are not rich enough to own your own 24 carat gold jewelry.

Gold's allure lies in its dual nature: it is both a tangible asset and a financial instrument. Throughout history, gold has been synonymous with wealth and power, making it a sought-after asset across cultures and eras. Today, gold continues to attract investors due to its resilience and ability to retain value during economic fluctuations. Knowledgeable traders who take positions in the gold market also benefit from this.

As you delve into gold trading, you'll discover the unique advantages it offers, such as liquidity, market depth, and opportunities for leverage.

THE DIFFERENCE BETWEEN INVESTING AND TRADING

Before we dive into the specifics, it's crucial to understand the distinction between investing in gold and trading gold online.

Investing typically involves purchasing physical gold or gold-backed assets to hold over a long period, with the expectation that their value will appreciate. This can include buying gold bars, coins, or shares in gold mining companies. The primary goal is wealth preservation and long-term capital appreciation.

Trading gold online, particularly through the forex market with gold currency pairs like XAU/USD, focuses on short-term market movements, aiming to profit from price fluctuations through various financial instruments.

These instruments include CFDs (Contracts for Difference), futures, options, and ETFs (Exchange-Traded Funds). Unlike traditional investing, trading gold in the forex market requires a more active approach, involving frequent buying and selling to capitalize on market trends and price swings.

This dynamic environment offers numerous opportunities but also demands a solid understanding of market mechanics and trading strategies. Trading gold currency pairs involves leveraging the volatility of gold prices against major currencies, allowing traders to exploit short-term price movements. Success in this arena requires keen market analysis, precise timing, and effective risk management.

WHO SHOULD TRADE GOLD?

Gold trading is not just for seasoned investors or financial experts. With the right knowledge and tools, anyone can start trading gold online. This book is designed for beginners who are eager to learn the ins and outs of the gold market and develop effective trading strategies.

Whether you are a student, a professional, or someone looking to supplement your income, this guide will provide you with the essential knowledge to start your journey in gold trading.

Gold trading can be particularly appealing for individuals who:

Seek Portfolio Diversification: Adding gold to your trading portfolio can reduce risk and improve returns by balancing more volatile assets like stocks.

Look for Safe-Haven Investments: In times of economic uncertainty, gold often acts as a safe haven, preserving value when other assets decline.

Enjoy Active Trading: If you thrive in fast-paced environments and enjoy analyzing market trends, gold trading offers ample opportunities for active participation and profit.

WHAT YOU CAN EXPECT FROM THIS BOOK

In the following chapters, you will find comprehensive information and practical advice on every aspect of gold trading. We'll start by exploring the historical significance of gold and its role in the modern financial system. This context will provide a foundation for understanding gold's intrinsic value and its behavior in different economic scenarios.

Next, we'll delve into the mechanics of the gold market, key trading platforms, and the fundamental and technical analysis techniques that will help you make informed trading decisions.

You'll learn how to interpret market signals, analyze price charts, and utilize various tools and indicators to predict gold price movements. We'll also cover essential topics like risk management, developing trading strategies, and staying updated with market news and trends.

By the end of this book, you will have a solid understanding of how to trade gold online, equipped with the knowledge and confidence to navigate the market effectively. The insights and strategies provided will empower you to make educated decisions, manage risks, and ultimately achieve your trading goals.

You will not grasp everything on the first read. This book can serve as your companion and refresher as you practice what you've learned, as well as a guide for further learning and reading.

Let's venture on this exciting journey together. Whether you're focused on expanding a strong trading portfolio or just delving into fresh financial opportunities, this guide will be your reliable ally in discovering the possibilities of trading gold online.

CHAPTER 2: THE HISTORY AND ALLURE OF PRECIOUS METALS

UNDERSTANDING THE TIMELESS APPEAL AND ENDURING VALUE OF GOLD

Gold has been a symbol of wealth and power for thousands of years. From ancient civilizations to modern economies, gold has played a pivotal role in shaping the course of history. In this chapter, we'll explore the fascinating history of gold, from its early use as currency to its status as a global standard of value.

GOLD IN ANCIENT CIVILIZATIONS

Gold's allure dates back to ancient times. The Egyptians were among the first to mine and utilize gold around 3000 BC, where it was used for jewelry, burial artifacts, and as a symbol of divine power. The famous tomb of Tutankhamun, filled with gold artifacts, exemplifies the reverence and value placed on gold.

The Greeks and Romans further cemented gold's role in society, using it for currency and establishing the first gold coins. In Rome, gold was central to the empire's economy, facilitating trade and commerce across vast territories. The enduring legacies of these civilizations highlight gold's historical importance.

THE MIDDLE AGES AND RENAISSANCE

During the Middle Ages, gold continued to be a key element of wealth and trade. The Byzantines and later European kingdoms hoarded gold, minting it into coins that fueled the economy. The Renaissance period saw an increased fascination with gold, not only for its economic value but also as a medium for art and architecture. Gold leaf and gilding became prominent in religious and secular art, symbolizing heavenly light and divine presence.

THE GOLD STANDARD AND MODERN ECONOMIES

The advent of the gold standard in the 19th century marked a significant turning point. Nations pegged their currencies to a specific amount of gold, ensuring stability and fostering international trade. The United States officially adopted the gold standard in 1879, with many other countries following suit. This system lasted until the mid-20th century, when economic pressures led to its gradual abandonment.

Despite the end of the gold standard, gold retained its status as a key reserve asset for central banks and a hedge against economic uncertainty. Its historical role as a reliable store of value continues to influence its modern-day significance.

GOLD IN THE MODERN ECONOMY

Despite the rise of digital currencies and other financial innovations, gold remains a vital component of the global economy. We'll examine the factors that contribute to gold's enduring appeal, including its role as a hedge against inflation and economic uncertainty. Understanding the unique properties of gold will help you appreciate why it continues to be a sought-after asset.

GOLD AS A HEDGE AGAINST INFLATION

Gold's ability to preserve wealth during times of inflation is one of its most compelling attributes. Unlike fiat currencies, which can lose value due to inflationary pressures, gold tends to retain its purchasing power. This characteristic makes gold an attractive asset during periods of high inflation or economic instability.

SAFE HAVEN ASSET

During times of geopolitical tension or financial market turbulence, investors often flock to gold as a safe haven. Its value tends to rise when confidence in other assets, such as stocks or bonds, diminishes. This behavior underscores gold's role as a stabilizing force in diversified investment portfolios.

INDUSTRIAL AND TECHNOLOGICAL USES

Beyond its monetary and investment roles, gold has practical applications in various industries. It is a critical component in electronics due to its excellent conductivity and resistance to corrosion. The medical field also utilizes gold in treatments and diagnostic procedures. These industrial uses contribute to steady demand, supporting gold's value in the modern economy.

CENTRAL BANK RESERVES

Central banks around the world hold significant gold reserves, reflecting its continued importance in the global financial system. These reserves provide a buffer against currency fluctuations and economic crises, highlighting gold's enduring role as a cornerstone of monetary policy.

THE EMOTIONAL AND CULTURAL APPEAL OF GOLD

Beyond its financial value, gold holds a special place in human culture and psychology. From its use in religious artifacts to its portrayal in art and literature, gold symbolizes purity, prosperity, and achievement. This chapter will delve into the cultural and emotional significance of gold, offering insights into why it captivates the human imagination.

RELIGIOUS AND SPIRITUAL SYMBOLISM

Gold has long been associated with the divine and the eternal. Many religions use gold in their rituals and artifacts, symbolizing purity, enlightenment, and immortality. In Christianity, gold is often used in church decorations and religious icons. In Hinduism, gold is associated with Lakshmi, the goddess of wealth and prosperity. These spiritual connotations add a layer of reverence to gold's value.

GOLD IN ART AND LITERATURE

Artists and writers have been inspired by gold for centuries. Gold's malleability and luster make it a favored material for sculptures, paintings, and manuscripts. The use of gold leaf in medieval manuscripts, Renaissance paintings, and even modern art illustrates its enduring appeal. Literature, from ancient myths to contemporary novels, often features gold as a symbol of wealth, power, and beauty.

CULTURAL TRADITIONS AND CELEBRATIONS

Gold plays a significant role in cultural traditions and celebrations worldwide. In many cultures, gold jewelry is a traditional gift for weddings, symbolizing prosperity and good fortune. Festivals like Diwali in India and Chinese New Year see a surge in gold purchases, reflecting its cultural significance.

PSYCHOLOGICAL IMPACT

Gold's visual appeal and intrinsic value evoke a psychological response that transcends its monetary worth. The sight of gold can elicit feelings of wealth, success, and security. This emotional connection enhances its desirability, making it more than just a financial asset.

Gold's historical significance, enduring economic value, and deep cultural and emotional appeal make it a unique and sought after asset.

Understanding these aspects provides a good foundation for appreciating the complexities and opportunities of gold trading, including what drives demand and price movements.

CHAPTER 3: WHAT THIS BOOK WILL TEACH YOU

MASTERING THE FUNDAMENTALS AND ADVANCED STRATEGIES OF GOLD TRADING

The gold market can seem complex and intimidating to beginners. This book aims to demystify the process of trading gold online, providing you with clear, step-by-step guidance. We'll cover everything from setting up your trading account to executing your first trade, ensuring you have a solid foundation to build upon.

Setting Up Your Trading Account: Learn how to choose a reliable broker, open a trading account, and navigate the platform interface. We will guide you through the process of depositing funds and understanding account types and their features.

Market Overview: Gain insights into how the gold market operates, including trading hours, key players, and the differences between various gold trading instruments such as spot gold, futures, and ETFs.

Executing Trades: Understand the mechanics of placing orders, including market orders, limit orders, and stop orders. We will provide a detailed walkthrough of executing your first trade, ensuring you are confident in the process.

Market Analysis: Learn the basics of market analysis, including how to read price charts, identify trends, and use technical indicators. We will introduce you to the tools and techniques used to analyze gold market data and make informed trading decisions.

ESSENTIAL TRADING STRATEGIES

Successful gold trading requires a combination of knowledge, skill, and strategy. We'll introduce you to a range of trading strategies, from short-term techniques like day trading and scalping to longer-term approaches like swing trading and trend following. Each strategy will be explained in detail, with practical examples to help you apply them effectively.

Day Trading: Discover how to capitalize on intraday price movements. Learn about the importance of timing, volatility, and liquidity in day trading. We will provide examples of day trading strategies and tips for success.

Scalping: Explore the fast-paced world of scalping, where traders seek to make small profits from numerous trades throughout the day. Understand the key principles of scalping and the tools needed to execute this strategy.

Swing Trading: Learn how to identify and trade market swings over several days or weeks. We will cover the techniques for spotting potential reversal points and managing positions to capture intermediate-term price movements.

Trend Following: Understand the strategy of riding established market trends. Learn how to use trend-following indicators and manage your trades to maximize profits while minimizing risks.

Fundamental Analysis: Incorporate fundamental analysis into your trading strategy. We will explain how to analyze economic data, geopolitical events, and other factors that impact gold prices.

RISK MANAGEMENT AND BEST PRACTICES

Trading gold online involves risks, but with the right approach, you can manage and mitigate them. This book will teach you essential risk management techniques, including setting stop-loss orders, diversifying your portfolio, and using leverage wisely. We'll also share best practices for maintaining discipline and avoiding common trading mistakes.

Stop-Loss Orders: Learn how to set stop-loss orders to protect your capital from significant losses. Understand the importance of risk-to-reward ratios and how to determine appropriate stop levels.

Diversification: Discover the benefits of diversifying your trading portfolio across different assets and markets. We will discuss various diversification strategies and how they can reduce overall risk.

Leverage Management: Understand the risks and rewards of using leverage in gold trading. Learn how to use leverage responsibly and avoid the pitfalls of over-leveraging your positions.

Psychological Discipline: Trading requires mental toughness and discipline. We will provide tips on how to maintain emotional control, stick to your trading plan, and avoid common psychological traps.

Common Mistakes to Avoid: Learn from the experiences of others by understanding the common mistakes made by novice traders. We will highlight these pitfalls and provide strategies to avoid them.

TOOLS AND RESOURCES FOR CONTINUED LEARNING

The world of gold trading is constantly evolving, with new tools, technologies, and market trends emerging all the time. In addition to the core content, this book will provide you with a wealth of resources for ongoing learning. From recommended reading lists to trusted news sources and educational platforms, you'll have everything you need to stay informed and ahead of the curve.

Trading Platforms and Software: Explore the various trading platforms and software available for gold traders. We will review their features, benefits, and how to choose the right one for your needs.

Market News and Analysis: Stay updated with the latest market news and analysis. We will recommend reliable sources for real-time data, expert commentary, and market insights.

Educational Resources: Continue your education with our list of recommended books, online courses, webinars, and forums. These resources will help you deepen your understanding of gold trading and keep your skills sharp.

Analytical Tools: Discover the tools and technologies that can enhance your trading efficiency. From charting software to automated trading systems, we will cover the essentials you need to succeed in the digital age of gold trading.

By the end of this book, you will have a solid understanding of how to trade gold online, equipped with the knowledge and confidence to navigate the market effectively. The insights and strategies provided will empower you to make educated decisions, manage risks, and ultimately achieve your trading goals.

Whether you are aiming to build a robust trading portfolio or simply explore new financial horizons, this guide will be your trusted companion in unlocking the potential of gold trading.

PART 2: THE BASICS OF GOLD TRADING

CHAPTER 4: HOW THE GOLD MARKET WORKS

UNDERSTANDING THE MECHANICS AND DYNAMICS OF GOLD TRADING

Understanding how the gold market operates is fundamental to becoming a successful trader. This chapter will provide you with an overview of the key components and mechanisms that drive the gold market.

THE STRUCTURE OF THE GOLD MARKET

The gold market consists of several interconnected components that facilitate the buying and selling of gold. These include physical gold markets, futures markets, and over-the-counter (OTC) markets.

Physical Gold Market: This involves the actual buying and selling of physical gold, such as bars, coins, and jewelry. Major physical gold markets are located in cities like London, Zurich, and Hong Kong. These markets are essential for setting benchmark prices and providing liquidity.

- **London Bullion Market:** The largest physical gold market globally, with the London Bullion Market Association (LBMA) setting the standards for gold purity and facilitating large-scale transactions between institutions.

- **Zurich:** Another major hub for gold trading, known for its robust financial infrastructure and secure storage facilities.
- **Hong Kong:** A crucial gateway for gold trading in Asia, providing a link between Western and Eastern markets.

Futures Market: The futures market allows traders to buy and sell contracts for the delivery of gold at a future date. These contracts are standardized and traded on exchanges such as the COMEX in New York and the Tokyo Commodity Exchange (TOCOM). Futures trading is crucial for price discovery and hedging.

- **COMEX:** Part of the CME Group, COMEX is the world's leading gold futures exchange, providing liquidity and setting global benchmark prices.
- **TOCOM:** Japan's premier futures exchange, offering gold futures contracts that play a significant role in the Asian gold market.

Over-the-Counter (OTC) Market: The OTC market is a decentralized market where gold is traded directly between parties, typically involving large institutions and bullion banks. This market provides flexibility and is less regulated than exchanges.

- **Flexibility:** OTC transactions can be customized to meet the specific needs of the parties involved, including terms of delivery, quantity, and price.
- **Participants:** The OTC market is primarily used by large institutions, central banks, and high-net-worth individuals seeking tailored transactions.

GOLD PRICING MECHANISMS

Gold prices are determined by supply and demand dynamics, influenced by various factors such as economic data, geopolitical events, and market sentiment.

Spot Price: The spot price is the current market price at which gold can be bought or sold for immediate delivery. It serves as a reference point for pricing gold futures and options.

- **Real-Time Data:** Spot prices are updated continuously during trading hours, reflecting real-time market conditions.
- **Global Benchmark:** Used by traders and investors worldwide to gauge the current value of gold.

Gold Fixing: The London Bullion Market Association (LBMA) conducts a gold fixing process twice daily, where a panel of major banks sets the gold price through a series of auctions. This price is used as a benchmark for pricing gold products.

- **Morning and Afternoon Fixes:** These fixes provide a snapshot of market conditions and help establish a consistent pricing reference.
- **Transparency:** The fixing process involves transparent auctions, ensuring that prices reflect the true market value.

Futures Prices: Futures prices reflect the market's expectations of future gold prices and include factors such as storage costs, interest rates, and market sentiment.

- **Forward Pricing:** Futures prices provide insights into market expectations and help traders make informed decisions.
- **Hedging Tool:** Used by producers and consumers to lock in prices and manage price risk.

KEY PARTICIPANTS IN THE GOLD MARKET

Understanding the roles of different market participants can provide insights into market dynamics.

Miners and Producers: Gold mining companies extract gold from the earth and supply it to the market. Their production levels can impact gold prices.

- **Major Producers:** Countries like China, Australia, and Russia are leading gold producers, influencing global supply.

- **Production Costs:** Factors such as extraction costs, environmental regulations, and geopolitical stability affect production levels and prices.

Bullion Banks: These are large banks that trade in physical gold and gold derivatives. They play a crucial role in providing liquidity and facilitating large transactions.

- **Market Makers:** Bullion banks act as intermediaries, buying and selling gold to maintain market liquidity.

- **Derivatives Trading:** They also engage in trading gold futures, options, and other derivatives to hedge risks and speculate on price movements.

Investors and Speculators: These participants include individual traders, hedge funds, and institutional investors who buy and sell gold to profit from price movements or hedge against risk.

- **Institutional Investors:** Pension funds, mutual funds, and hedge funds often include gold in their portfolios for diversification and hedging purposes.

- **Retail Traders:** Individual traders and small investors participate in the market through online trading platforms, buying and selling gold ETFs, futures, and CFDs.

Jewelers and Industrial Users: These participants purchase gold for manufacturing jewelry and industrial applications, contributing to the demand side of the market.

- **Jewelry Demand:** Jewelry remains one of the largest consumers of gold, particularly in countries like India and China.
- **Industrial Uses:** Gold's unique properties make it valuable in electronics, dentistry, and aerospace applications.

This may seem like a lot to take in, but as you experience the market, you will become more familiar with the dynamics that drive price movements. By understanding the structure and key components of the gold market, traders can navigate this complex environment more effectively. Knowledge of the various market participants and pricing mechanisms provides a solid foundation for making informed trading decisions.

As you delve deeper into gold trading, this understanding will serve as a critical tool in your trading arsenal, enabling you to capitalize on market opportunities and manage risks proficiently.

CHAPTER 5: KEY TERMS AND CONCEPTS IN GOLD TRADING

BUILDING YOUR GOLD TRADING VOCABULARY

To trade gold effectively, you need to be familiar with the key terms and concepts used in the market. This chapter will introduce you to the essential vocabulary and principles of gold trading, providing you with the foundation needed to navigate the market confidently.

COMMON GOLD TRADING TERMS

Bid/Ask Price: The bid price is the highest price a buyer is willing to pay for gold, while the ask price is the lowest price a seller is willing to accept. The difference between the two is known as the spread. Understanding this spread is crucial as it impacts the cost of trading and your potential profits.

- **Bid Price Example:** If the bid price for gold is $1,800 per ounce, buyers are willing to pay up to that amount.

- **Ask Price Example:** If the ask price is $1,802 per ounce, sellers are willing to accept at least that amount to sell their gold.

Pip (Percentage in Point): A pip is a unit of measurement used to express the change in value between two currencies or commodities. In gold trading, it often represents the smallest price movement. For example, if the price of gold moves from $1,800.00 to

$1,800.10, it has moved 10 pips.

Leverage: Leverage allows traders to control a large position with a relatively small amount of capital. It amplifies both potential gains and losses. For instance, with 10:1 leverage, a $1,000 investment can control $10,000 worth of gold.

Margin: Margin is the amount of money required to open and maintain a leveraged trading position.

- **Initial Margin:** The amount needed to open a trade. For example, if you need $1,000 to open a $10,000 position with 10:1 leverage, $1,000 is your initial margin.

- **Maintenance Margin:** The minimum amount that must be maintained in your account to keep a trade open. If your account falls below this level, a margin call occurs, and you may need to add more funds to avoid closing your position.

CFD (Contract for Difference): A CFD is a financial derivative that allows traders to speculate on the price movement of gold without owning the physical asset. Profits and losses are based on the difference between the opening and closing prices of the contract. CFDs offer flexibility and leverage but also come with higher risk.

FUNDAMENTAL CONCEPTS

Support and Resistance:

Support Levels: Price points where a downward trend is expected to pause due to a concentration of demand. For example, if gold prices fall to $1,750 and repeatedly bounce back up, $1,750 is a support level.

Resistance Levels: Price points where an upward trend is expected to pause due to a concentration of supply. For instance, if gold prices rise to $1,850 and struggle to break through, $1,850 is a resistance level.

Trend Lines:

Uptrend: Characterized by higher highs and higher lows. Drawing a trend line along the lows of the uptrend helps identify support levels.

Downtrend: Characterized by lower highs and lower lows. Drawing a trend line along the highs of the downtrend helps identify resistance levels.

Moving Averages: Moving averages smooth out price data to identify the direction of the trend.

Simple Moving Average (SMA): Calculated by averaging the closing prices over a specific period. For example, a 50-day SMA adds the closing prices of the past 50 days and divides by 50.

Exponential Moving Average (EMA): Gives more weight to recent prices, making it more responsive to new information. A 50-day EMA will react more quickly to price changes than a 50-day SMA.

Volatility: Volatility measures the degree of variation in gold prices over a period of time.

High Volatility: Indicates significant price movements and potential trading opportunities but also higher risk.

Low Volatility: Indicates stable prices and potentially fewer trading opportunities, but lower risk.

RISK MANAGEMENT

Stop-Loss Order: A stop-loss order automatically closes a trade at a predetermined price to limit potential losses. For example, if you buy gold at $1,800, you might set a stop-loss order at $1,750 to cap your loss at $50 per ounce.

Take-Profit Order: A take-profit order automatically closes a trade at a predetermined profit level. If you buy gold at $1,800 and set a take-profit order at $1,850, your trade will close when the price reaches $1,850, securing your profit.

Risk-to-Reward Ratio: This ratio compares the potential profit of a trade to the potential loss. A higher ratio indicates a more favorable trade setup. For instance, if you're willing to risk $100 to make $300, your risk-to-reward ratio is 1:3.

Example: If you set a stop-loss order at $1,750 and a take-profit order at $1,850 when buying at $1,800, your risk is $50, and your reward is $50, resulting in a 1:1 risk-to-reward ratio.

By familiarizing yourself with these key terms and concepts, you'll be better equipped to navigate the gold market and make informed trading decisions. This foundational knowledge will help you understand market dynamics, execute trades effectively, and manage risks to enhance your trading performance.

CHAPTER 6: MAJOR GOLD TRADING PLATFORMS AND MARKETS

NAVIGATING THE HUBS OF GLOBAL GOLD TRADING

Selecting the right trading platform and understanding the major gold markets are crucial steps in your trading journey. This chapter will guide you through the top platforms and markets for trading gold online, providing you with the knowledge to make informed decisions about where and how to trade.

ONLINE TRADING PLATFORMS

MetaTrader 4 (MT4):

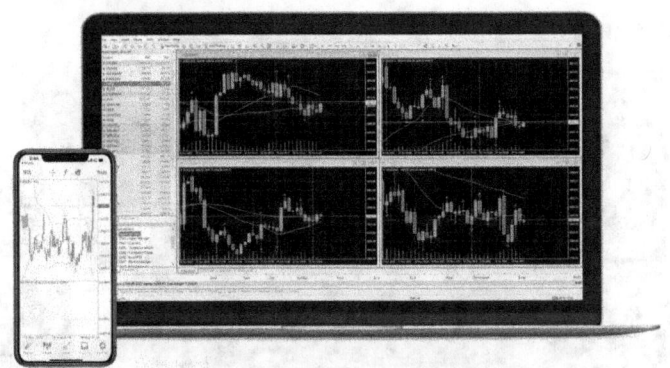

Trading Platform: cmcmarkets.com. MT4 and MT5 have the same user interface, the difference being that MT 5 has more features.

Overview: MT4 is a popular trading platform known for its user-friendly interface and powerful analytical tools. It supports automated trading through Expert Advisors (EAs).

Features: Advanced charting capabilities, a wide range of technical indicators, and support for multiple trading orders. MT4 also offers backtesting capabilities for EAs and a robust security system.

Benefits: Suitable for both beginners and experienced traders, offering a vast online community and extensive resources for learning and support.

MetaTrader 5 (MT5):

Overview: MT5 offers additional features compared to MT4, including more timeframes, advanced charting tools, and an integrated economic calendar.

Features: Depth of Market (DOM) feature, more order types (such as buy stop limit and sell stop limit), and improved charting tools.

Benefits: Ideal for traders looking for a more comprehensive trading platform with enhanced analytical tools and capabilities.

TradingView:

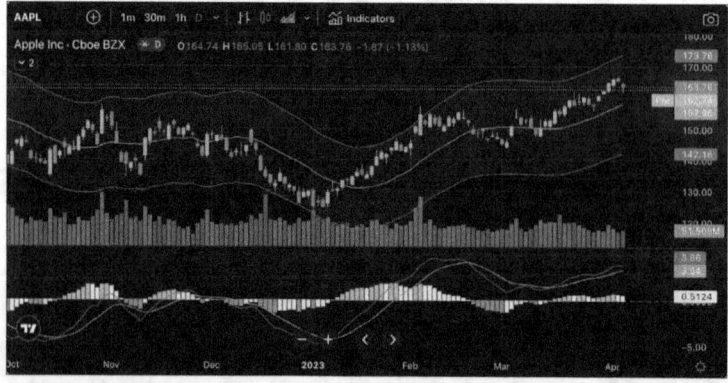

TradingView Desktop Application: tradingview.com

Overview: TradingView is a web-based platform that provides advanced charting tools and a social trading community. It is ideal for traders who value technical analysis.

Features: Extensive range of chart types, over 100 technical indicators, and the ability to create custom indicators. TradingView also supports collaborative features like sharing charts and trading ideas.

Benefits: Excellent for traders who prefer a visually intuitive platform and enjoy engaging with a community of traders to share insights and strategies.

cTrader:

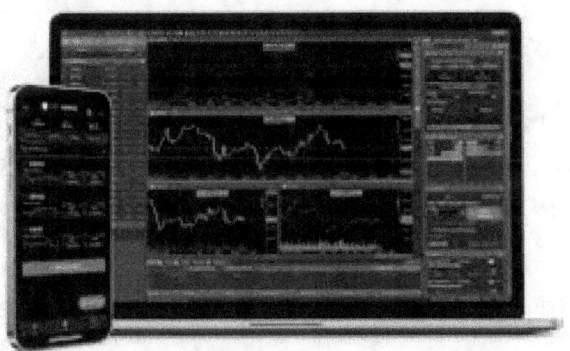

cTrader Platform: fpmarkets.com

Overview: cTrader is known for its intuitive interface and fast execution speeds. It offers advanced order types and comprehensive charting capabilities.

Features: Direct Market Access (DMA), one-click trading, Level II pricing, and algorithmic trading support via cAlgo (the programming language used for development on the cTrader platform).

Benefits: Ideal for traders who prioritize execution speed and advanced order functionality, providing a transparent trading environment.

MAJOR GOLD MARKETS

London Bullion Market (LBMA):

Overview: The LBMA is the largest global market for OTC gold trading. It sets the standard for gold purity and facilitates large transactions between bullion banks and institutional participants.

Key Features: The LBMA Gold Price, which serves as a benchmark for global gold prices, and the Good Delivery List, which sets the standards for the quality and weight of gold bars.

Importance: The LBMA plays a critical role in maintaining market integrity and liquidity, influencing gold prices worldwide.

New York Mercantile Exchange (NYMEX):

Overview: Part of the CME Group, NYMEX is a leading futures exchange where gold futures and options are traded. It plays a key role in price discovery and risk management.

Key Features: Standardized gold futures contracts, options on futures, and electronic trading via the CME Globex platform.

Importance: NYMEX is vital for hedging and speculative activities, offering liquidity and transparency in gold pricing.

Shanghai Gold Exchange (SGE):

Overview: The SGE is China's primary gold trading platform, offering both spot and futures contracts. It is a significant player in the global gold market, reflecting China's substantial demand for gold.

Key Features: Physical gold trading, gold leasing, and gold futures trading. The SGE also sets the Shanghai Gold Benchmark Price.

Importance: The SGE's influence on global gold prices is growing, particularly as China is a major consumer and producer of gold.

Tokyo Commodity Exchange (TOCOM):

Overview: TOCOM is Japan's premier futures exchange, offering gold futures contracts. It is an important hub for gold trading in Asia.

Key Features: Standardized futures contracts, options on futures, and a variety of trading instruments for hedging and speculative purposes.

Importance: TOCOM provides crucial liquidity and price discovery for gold in the Asian markets, impacting regional and global gold prices.

CHOOSING THE RIGHT PLATFORM

When selecting a trading platform, consider the following factors:

Ease of Use:

Considerations: Choose a platform with a user-friendly interface that suits your level of experience. For beginners, platforms like MT4 or TradingView offer intuitive navigation and extensive educational resources.

Analytical Tools:

Considerations: Ensure the platform offers robust charting tools, technical indicators, and real-time data. Platforms like MT5 and TradingView excel in providing advanced analytical capabilities.

Execution Speed:

Considerations: Fast execution speeds are essential for capitalizing on market opportunities and minimizing slippage. cTrader is known for its rapid execution and direct market access.

Regulation and Security:

Considerations: Select a platform that is regulated by a reputable authority and provides secure trading environments. Platforms like MT4 and MT5 are widely used and supported by regulated brokers.

Customer Support:

Considerations: Reliable customer support can help you resolve issues quickly and efficiently. Look for platforms with strong support infrastructure, including live chat, phone support, and comprehensive FAQs.

By mastering the basics of gold trading and choosing the right platform and market, you'll be well-prepared to navigate the market and make informed trading decisions. In the next part, we will delve deeper into market analysis techniques and strategies to enhance your trading skills.

PART 3: ANALYZING THE GOLD MARKET

CHAPTER 7: FACTORS INFLUENCING GOLD PRICES

UNDERSTANDING THE DRIVERS OF GOLD MARKET DYNAMICS

Understanding the factors that influence gold prices is crucial for successful gold trading. In this chapter, we'll explore the key elements that drive gold prices and how you can use this knowledge to your advantage.

SUPPLY AND DEMAND DYNAMICS

Mining Production:

Overview: The amount of gold produced by mining operations directly impacts the supply side of the market. Major producers include countries like China, Australia, and Russia, which collectively account for a significant portion of global gold production.

Influence on Prices: Any significant changes in mining production, such as strikes, natural disasters, or technological advancements, can influence gold prices. For example, a decrease in production due to a strike can reduce supply, potentially driving prices higher.

Jewelry and Industrial Demand:

Jewelry Demand: Gold's primary use in jewelry accounts for a significant portion of its demand. Countries like India and China are major consumers, where gold jewelry holds cultural significance.

Industrial Demand: Gold is also used in various industrial applications, including electronics, dentistry, and aerospace. Technological advancements that increase the use of gold in industry can boost demand.

Impact on Prices: High demand in jewelry and industrial sectors often supports gold prices. For instance, during festive seasons in India, the demand for gold jewelry typically increases, leading to a rise in prices.

GEOPOLITICAL EVENTS

Political Instability:

Safe-Haven Asset: Gold is often seen as a safe-haven asset during times of political uncertainty. Investors flock to gold to preserve their wealth when facing events like elections, conflicts, and policy changes.

Examples: Events such as Brexit, the US-China trade war, and conflicts in the Middle East have historically led to spikes in gold prices as investors seek stability.

Economic Sanctions:

Impact on Producers: Sanctions on gold-producing countries or disruptions in the global supply chain can affect gold prices by creating supply constraints.

Case Study: Sanctions imposed on countries like Iran have impacted their ability to trade gold internationally, leading to fluctuations in global gold prices.

MONETARY POLICY

Interest Rates:

Central Banks: Central banks' interest rate policies can significantly influence gold prices. Lower interest rates reduce the opportunity cost of holding gold, often leading to higher prices.

Mechanism: When interest rates are low, the return on investments like bonds becomes less attractive compared to gold, prompting investors to shift their capital to gold.

Quantitative Easing:

Definition: Policies like quantitative easing, where central banks inject money into the economy, can devalue fiat currencies and increase the attractiveness of gold as an alternative investment.

Historical Context: During the 2008 financial crisis, the US Federal Reserve implemented quantitative easing, which led to a significant increase in gold prices as the dollar weakened.

INFLATION AND CURRENCY FLUCTUATIONS

Inflation Rates:

Hedge Against Inflation: Gold is often used as a hedge against inflation. Rising inflation erodes the value of fiat currencies, leading investors to seek the relative stability of gold.

Example: In periods of high inflation, such as the 1970s in the US, gold prices surged as investors sought protection against the declining purchasing power of the dollar.

Currency Strength:

US Dollar Relationship: Gold prices are inversely related to the strength of the US dollar. When the dollar weakens, gold prices generally rise, and vice versa.

Dynamics: A strong dollar makes gold more expensive for holders of other currencies, reducing demand. Conversely, a weak dollar makes gold cheaper for foreign buyers, increasing demand.

By understanding these factors—supply and demand dynamics, geopolitical events, monetary policy, and inflation and currency fluctuations—you will be better equipped to anticipate and react to changes in gold prices.

This knowledge is a vital component of developing effective trading strategies and making informed decisions in the gold market. In the next chapter, we will delve into the impact of various economic indicators on gold prices, further enhancing your analytical skills.

CHAPTER 8: ECONOMIC INDICATORS AND THEIR IMPACT ON GOLD

DECIPHERING THE SIGNALS THAT DRIVE GOLD PRICES

Economic indicators are crucial tools for understanding the health of the economy and predicting its future trajectory. In this chapter, we'll delve into the most important economic indicators and how they influence gold prices.

GROSS DOMESTIC PRODUCT (GDP)

Definition: GDP measures the total economic output of a country over a specific period, usually quarterly or annually. It encompasses all goods and services produced within the country's borders and is a key indicator of economic health.

Impact on Gold:

Strong GDP Growth: Robust GDP growth signals a healthy economy, boosting investor confidence and appetite for riskier assets. This can lead to higher interest rates and a stronger currency, making gold less attractive as an investment compared to other assets.

Weak GDP Growth: Conversely, sluggish or negative GDP growth prompts investors to seek safe-haven assets like gold to protect their wealth against economic uncertainty. In such scenarios, gold prices tend to rise as demand increases.

INFLATION RATES

Consumer Price Index (CPI) and Producer Price Index (PPI):

CPI: The Consumer Price Index measures changes in the price level of a basket of consumer goods and services, reflecting inflationary pressures on households.

PPI: The Producer Price Index measures the average changes in selling prices received by domestic producers for their output, offering insights into inflation at the production level.

Impact on Gold:

High Inflation: When inflation rates rise, the purchasing power of fiat currencies declines. As a result, investors turn to gold as a hedge against inflation, driving up demand and prices.

Inflation Expectations: Anticipation of future inflation can also influence gold prices. Central bank policies and economic data indicating potential inflationary pressures can lead investors to allocate more capital to gold.

EMPLOYMENT DATA

Non-Farm Payrolls (NFP) and Unemployment Rate:

NFP: The Non-Farm Payrolls report provides data on the number of jobs added or lost in the US economy, excluding the farming sector, offering insights into overall employment trends.

Unemployment Rate: This percentage reflects the proportion of the labor force that is unemployed and actively seeking employment.

Impact on Gold:

Strong Employment Data: Positive employment data can signal a robust economy, potentially prompting central banks to raise interest rates to prevent overheating. Higher interest rates typically strengthen the domestic currency and reduce the appeal of gold, leading to lower prices.

Weak Employment Data: Conversely, weak employment figures may prompt central banks to adopt accommodative monetary policies, such as lowering interest rates or implementing stimulus measures. This can weaken the domestic currency and boost gold prices as investors seek safe-haven assets.

MONETARY POLICY ANNOUNCEMENTS

Federal Reserve Meetings and Central Bank Statements:

Federal Reserve: The decisions and statements of the US Federal Reserve on interest rates and monetary policy have a significant impact on financial markets worldwide, including the gold market.

Other Central Banks: Statements and policies from major central banks like the European Central Bank (ECB) and the Bank of Japan (BOJ) also influence investor sentiment and market dynamics.

Impact on Gold:

Hawkish Monetary Policy: When central banks adopt a hawkish stance by tightening monetary policy (e.g., raising interest rates), it can bolster confidence in the economy and strengthen the domestic currency. This typically diminishes the appeal of gold as an alternative investment, leading to lower prices.

Dovish Monetary Policy: Conversely, a dovish stance (e.g., lowering interest rates or implementing quantitative easing) tends to weaken the currency and increase demand for gold as a hedge against currency depreciation and inflation. This often drives gold prices higher.

Understanding the interplay between these economic indicators and gold prices is essential for formulating informed trading strategies and navigating the complexities of the gold market. In the next chapter, we'll explore the methodologies of technical and fundamental analysis and how they can be applied to gold trading.

CHAPTER 9: TECHNICAL ANALYSIS

CHARTING TRENDS AND PREDICTING MARKET MOVEMENTS

Technical analysis is a method of evaluating securities by analyzing statistical trends gathered from trading activity, such as price movement and volume. Traders use various tools and techniques to interpret market data and make informed trading decisions. One of the core aspects of technical analysis is the study of chart patterns.

1. CHART PATTERNS

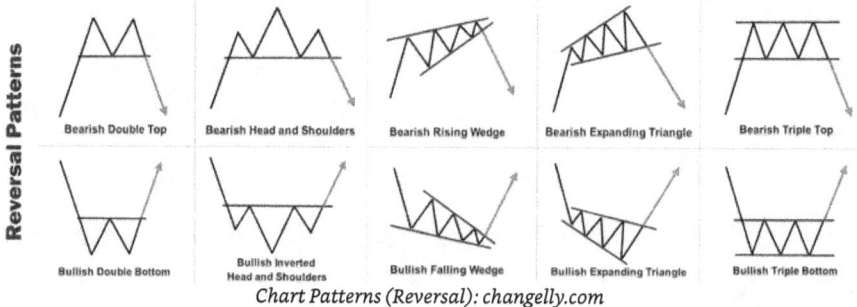

Chart Patterns (Reversal): changelly.com

Technical analysts study price charts to identify recurring patterns that may indicate future price movements. These patterns are formed by the price actions of the underlying asset and can provide valuable insights into market psychology and potential price directions.

Common chart patterns include:

Head and Shoulders: This pattern typically signals a reversal in trend. It consists of three peaks: the middle peak (head) being the highest and two lower peaks (shoulders) on either side. An inverse head and shoulders pattern signals a reversal from a downtrend to an uptrend.

Double Tops and Bottoms: A double top is a bearish reversal pattern that forms after a price reaches a high point twice with a moderate decline between the two peaks. Conversely, a double bottom is a bullish reversal pattern that occurs after a price hits a low point twice with a moderate rise in between.

Triangles: Triangles can be ascending, descending, or symmetrical. An ascending triangle, characterized by a horizontal top and rising bottom, suggests a potential upward breakout. A descending triangle, with a horizontal bottom and descending top, indicates a possible downward breakout. A symmetrical triangle, formed by converging trendlines, can break out in either direction.

Application:

Recognizing these patterns can help traders anticipate potential market reversals or continuations. Here's how traders typically apply chart patterns in their analysis:

Identify Patterns: Traders closely monitor price charts to spot emerging patterns. Tools like trendlines, moving averages, and other charting tools help in visualizing these patterns.

Confirm Patterns: Before acting on a pattern, traders seek confirmation. This could involve waiting for a breakout above resistance (in the case of bullish patterns) or below support (for bearish patterns). Volume analysis often accompanies pattern confirmation, with increased trading volume providing stronger validation of the pattern.

Set Entry and Exit Points: Once a pattern is confirmed, traders set entry points to capitalize on the anticipated price movement. For instance, entering a long position on a confirmed inverse head and shoulders or a short position on a double top. Exit points, often based on the pattern's projected price target, help manage risk and lock in profits.

Use Stop-Loss Orders: To mitigate risk, traders use stop-loss orders, placing them just below (for long positions) or above (for short positions) key levels identified by the pattern. This helps limit potential losses if the market moves against the trade.

2. INDICATORS AND OSCILLATORS:

Technical analysts utilize a variety of indicators and oscillators to analyze price trends and market momentum. These tools provide insights into the strength and direction of trends, helping traders make more informed decisions about entry and exit points.

Tools

Indicators and oscillators are essential components of technical analysis, each serving a specific purpose in evaluating market conditions.

Moving Averages (MA):

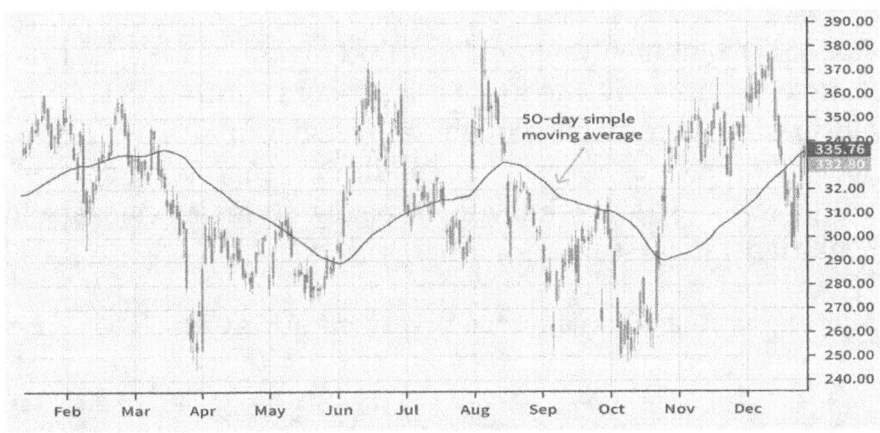

Simple Moving Average (SMA): investopedia.com

Moving averages smooth out price data to create a trend-following indicator. There are two main types: simple moving averages (SMA), which calculate the average price over a specified period, and exponential moving averages (EMA), which give more weight to recent prices. Moving averages help identify the direction of the trend and can be used to generate buy and sell signals when prices cross above or below the moving average.

Relative Strength Index (RSI):

Relative Strength Index (RSI) bottom chart. commodity.com

The RSI is a momentum oscillator that measures the speed and change of price movements on a scale from 0 to 100. It is typically used to identify overbought or oversold conditions. An RSI above 70 indicates overbought conditions, suggesting a potential price correction, while an RSI below 30 indicates oversold conditions, suggesting a potential price rise.

Moving Average Convergence Divergence (MACD):

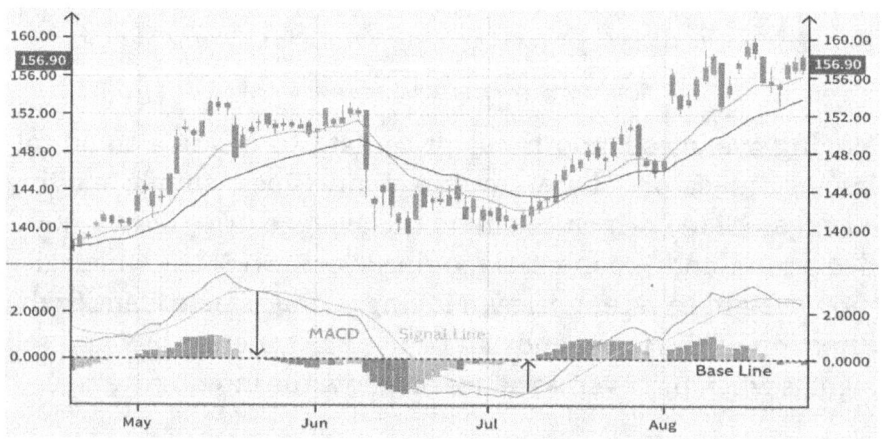

Moving Average Convergence Divergence (MACD): investopedia.com

The MACD is a trend-following momentum indicator that shows the relationship between two moving averages of a security's price. The MACD is calculated by subtracting the 26-period EMA from the 12-period EMA. A signal line (9-period EMA of the MACD) is then plotted on top of the MACD line, which can generate buy or sell signals when crossed. The MACD histogram, which plots the difference between the MACD line and the signal line, helps in identifying the strength of the trend.

Purpose

These tools help traders identify overbought or oversold conditions and potential entry or exit points. Here's how they are typically used:

Identifying Trends: Moving averages are used to identify the direction of the trend. If the price is above the moving average, it indicates an uptrend, and if it is below, it indicates a downtrend. The crossover of shorter and longer moving averages can signal the start or end of a trend.

Overbought and Oversold Conditions: Oscillators like the RSI help traders determine whether an asset is overbought or oversold. In overbought conditions, prices are likely to reverse downwards, and in oversold conditions, they are likely to reverse upwards. This information helps traders anticipate potential reversals and take advantage of market corrections.

Entry and Exit Points: Indicators such as the MACD provide signals for potential entry and exit points. When the MACD line crosses above the signal line, it generates a buy signal, and when it crosses below, it generates a sell signal. The histogram helps gauge the strength of the signal.

Confirmation of Patterns: Indicators and oscillators can be used to confirm chart patterns and other technical analysis signals. For example, if a bullish pattern is identified on the chart, a corresponding bullish signal from the RSI or MACD adds confirmation and increases the reliability of the trade.

Divergence Analysis: Divergence occurs when the price of an asset moves in the opposite direction of an indicator. For instance, if the price is making higher highs while the RSI is making lower highs, it indicates a potential reversal. Divergence analysis helps traders spot early signs of trend changes.

3. SUPPORT AND RESISTANCE LEVELS:

Support and resistance: dailyfx.com

Support and resistance levels are key concepts in technical analysis that refer to specific price levels where buying or selling pressure tends to be concentrated. These levels act as psychological barriers where the price of an asset tends to stop and reverse direction.

Support Level: A support level is a price level where a downtrend can be expected to pause due to a concentration of demand. As the price drops towards the support level, buyers become more likely to buy, preventing the price from falling further. It is the price floor that a security frequently hits but does not fall below for a certain period.

Resistance Level: A resistance level is a price level where an uptrend can be expected to pause due to a concentration of supply. As the price rises towards the resistance level, sellers become more likely to sell, preventing the price from rising further. It is the price ceiling that a security frequently hits but does not rise above for a certain period.

Identifying support and resistance levels helps traders make informed decisions about entry and exit points, as well as setting stop-loss and take-profit orders. Recognizing these levels is crucial for predicting price movements and managing risk.

Entry Points: Traders can enter long positions when the price approaches a support level, expecting the price to bounce back up. Conversely, they can enter short positions when the price approaches a resistance level, expecting the price to drop.

Exit Points: Traders can use support and resistance levels to set exit points for their trades. For example, they might close a long position near a resistance level or close a short position near a support level to secure profits.

Stop-Loss Orders: Placing stop-loss orders just below a support level for long positions or just above a resistance level for short positions can help manage risk. This strategy ensures that losses are minimized if the price moves against the trader's expectations.

Take-Profit Orders: Setting take-profit orders near support or resistance levels helps lock in profits when the price reaches these anticipated levels.

Advantages:

Visual Representation: Technical analysis provides a visual representation of market activity, making it easier to interpret price movements. Charting support and resistance levels on a price chart helps traders visually identify these key areas, facilitating better trading decisions.

Timing Trades: Technical analysis, particularly the use of support and resistance levels, is effective for short-term trading strategies. It allows traders to time their trades based on short-term price patterns and indicators, which is crucial for day trading or swing trading where quick decision-making is essential.

Application:
Using support and resistance levels involves several techniques and strategies to maximize their effectiveness:

Identifying Levels: Traders identify support and resistance levels by looking at historical price data. Horizontal lines are drawn on the price chart at levels where the price has previously reversed direction multiple times.

Role Reversal: Once a support level is broken, it often becomes a new resistance level, and vice versa. This phenomenon is known as role reversal and is a powerful concept in technical analysis. Understanding this can help traders anticipate future price movements.

Trend Lines: In addition to horizontal levels, trend lines can also act as dynamic support or resistance levels. Drawing trend lines that connect successive higher lows in an uptrend or lower highs in a downtrend can help identify areas where the price may reverse.

Zones vs. Lines: Instead of focusing on precise lines, traders often consider support and resistance zones. These are broader areas where price action is likely to encounter buying or selling pressure. This approach accounts for the fact that prices often fluctuate around these levels rather than stopping exactly at a specific price point.

Combining with Other Indicators: Support and resistance levels are most effective when used in conjunction with other technical analysis tools such as moving averages, MACD, RSI, and candlestick patterns. This multi-faceted approach increases the accuracy of predictions and enhances trading decisions.

Mastering technical analysis empowers traders to approach gold trading with confidence and precision. By harnessing the insights gleaned from charts, patterns, and indicators, traders can refine their trading strategies and adapt to changing market conditions.

As we move forward into the realm of fundamental analysis in the next chapter, remember that a well-rounded understanding of both technical and fundamental factors will be your cornerstone for making informed decisions in the dynamic world of gold trading.

CHAPTER 10: FUNDAMENTAL ANALYSIS

EXPLORING GOLD TRADING FACTORS

Fundamental analysis plays a crucial role in understanding the broader economic, geopolitical, and industrial factors that influence the price of gold. Unlike technical analysis, which focuses on historical price patterns and market psychology, fundamental analysis dives into the underlying economic and political forces driving supply and demand dynamics in the gold market.

In this chapter, we will explore how economic indicators, geopolitical events, and company performance impact gold prices. By gaining insights into these fundamental factors, traders can make informed decisions, anticipate market trends, and navigate the complexities of the gold market with confidence. Understanding fundamental analysis is essential for developing comprehensive trading strategies that consider both short-term market movements and long-term trends.

ECONOMIC INDICATORS:

Fundamental analysts delve into economic indicators such as GDP (Gross Domestic Product), inflation rates, and employment statistics to gauge the overall health of an economy and its potential impact on gold prices. These indicators offer insights into economic growth, consumer purchasing power, and inflationary pressures, all of which influence investor sentiment towards gold as a safe-haven asset or inflation hedge.

Significance: Changes in economic indicators can signal shifts in monetary policy by central banks, affecting interest rates and currency values, which in turn impact gold prices. For instance, high inflation rates may drive investors towards gold as a store of value, while strong GDP growth might lead to expectations of higher interest rates, potentially dampening gold's appeal.

GEOPOLITICAL EVENTS:

Fundamental analysts closely monitor geopolitical developments such as elections, geopolitical tensions, and trade disputes, as these events can create uncertainties that influence market sentiment and drive demand for gold as a perceived safe-haven asset.

Impact: Events like elections, conflicts, and international trade negotiations can trigger volatility in financial markets, prompting investors to seek refuge in gold due to its historical role as a hedge against geopolitical risk. Sudden geopolitical tensions can lead to increased demand for gold, driving prices higher irrespective of economic fundamentals.

COMPANY PERFORMANCE:

Investors in gold mining stocks assess the financial health and operational efficiency of mining companies. Key considerations include production costs, reserve estimates, management expertise, and exploration success rates.

Factors: Fundamental analysis of gold mining companies involves evaluating profitability margins, debt levels, capital expenditures, and dividend policies. Strong company performance and efficient management practices can enhance investor confidence and drive stock prices higher, influencing overall market sentiment towards gold investments.

ADVANTAGES:

Fundamental analysis provides a comprehensive view of market conditions, encompassing long-term economic trends and potential catalysts that could impact gold prices. This broader perspective helps investors and traders make informed decisions about entry and exit points based on fundamental factors.

Long-Term Strategies: Fundamental analysis is particularly valuable for investors employing long-term investment strategies. By identifying undervalued assets or companies with strong growth prospects, investors can position themselves to benefit from potential price appreciation over time. Understanding macroeconomic trends and fundamental market drivers enables investors to align their investment decisions with broader economic conditions.

Mastering fundamental analysis is an essential skill for any serious gold trader. By staying informed about economic indicators, geopolitical events, and the financial health of gold-related companies, traders can gain a deeper understanding of market dynamics and make informed trading decisions.

In the next chapter, we will explore how to integrate fundamental analysis with technical analysis to develop a more holistic approach to trading gold effectively. This synergy will enable traders to navigate various market conditions more confidently and seize opportunities aligned with their trading strategies.

CHAPTER 11: COMBINING TECHNICAL AND FUNDAMENTAL ANALYSIS

SYNERGIZING MARKET INSIGHTS FOR INFORMED TRADING DECISIONS

Successful traders often adopt a dual approach by combining technical and fundamental analysis to gain a more comprehensive understanding of the gold market. While technical analysis focuses on price patterns and market sentiment, fundamental analysis provides insights into broader economic factors and geopolitical events that influence gold prices.

Example: A trader might utilize fundamental analysis to identify long-term trends and potential market-moving events. For instance, they may monitor economic indicators like GDP growth rates, inflation data, and central bank policies to gauge the overall health of the economy and anticipate shifts in investor sentiment towards gold.

Concurrently, technical analysis tools such as moving averages, trend lines, and oscillators can be employed to pinpoint precise entry and exit points based on short-term price movements and market psychology.

By integrating these two approaches, traders can leverage the strengths of each method to enhance their decision-making process:

Identifying Market Trends: Fundamental analysis helps traders identify overarching trends in the gold market, such as periods of economic expansion or contraction, shifts in inflation expectations, or geopolitical tensions that could impact global financial stability. Understanding these trends allows traders to adopt a strategic long-term outlook and position themselves accordingly.

Fine-tuning Entry and Exit Points: Technical analysis complements fundamental insights by providing specific entry and exit signals based on price action and historical data. Traders can use technical indicators to confirm or refine their trading decisions, ensuring they enter positions at optimal points and manage risk effectively.

BENEFITS OF INTEGRATION:

Enhanced Decision-Making: Integrating technical and fundamental analysis provides a more robust framework for decision-making, offering a deeper understanding of market dynamics and potential catalysts that may drive price movements.

Adaptability to Market Conditions: By combining both approaches, traders are better equipped to adapt to changing market conditions. They can capitalize on short-term trading opportunities identified through technical analysis while maintaining awareness of longer-term trends and fundamental drivers.

Risk Management: The synergy between technical and fundamental analysis supports more informed risk management strategies. Traders can set stop-loss orders and manage position sizes based on both technical levels and fundamental factors, reducing exposure to unexpected market volatility.

Application: Implementing a combined approach involves:

Integration of Tools: Utilizing a blend of technical indicators (e.g., moving averages, RSI, MACD) alongside fundamental research into economic data and geopolitical events.

Continuous Analysis: Regularly updating analyses based on new information and market developments to refine trading strategies and adapt to evolving market conditions.

By mastering the integration of technical and fundamental analysis, traders can develop a holistic approach to gold trading that enhances their ability to identify profitable opportunities and navigate the complexities of the global financial markets effectively.

In the next part, we will delve into the practical aspects of getting started with gold trading, including setting up your trading account and choosing a broker.

PART 4: GETTING STARTED WITH GOLD TRADING

CHAPTER 12: SETTING UP YOUR TRADING ACCOUNT

ESSENTIAL STEPS AND CONSIDERATIONS FOR NEW TRADERS

Setting up your trading account is the first step in your journey to trading gold. This chapter will guide you through the process, ensuring you have everything you need to start trading effectively.

SELECTING A TRADING PLATFORM:

Choosing the right trading platform is crucial for your trading experience and success. There are several types of platforms available, each with its own set of features and benefits.

Platform Types:

Desktop Platforms: These are downloadable applications that you install on your computer. They often offer the most comprehensive set of features, including advanced charting tools, custom indicators, and automated trading capabilities. Examples include MetaTrader 4 (MT4) and MetaTrader 5 (MT5).

Web-Based Platforms: These platforms can be accessed through your internet browser without the need for installation. They offer the convenience of trading from any computer with internet access and are generally user-friendly. Examples include TradingView and cTrader.

Mobile Platforms: Designed for smartphones and tablets, these platforms allow you to trade on the go. They are ideal for traders who need to monitor and manage their trades from anywhere. Most major trading platforms offer mobile versions, such as MT4 and MT5 mobile apps.

Features to Consider:

Real-Time Data: Ensure the platform provides real-time price quotes and market data to make informed trading decisions.

Advanced Charting Tools: Look for platforms with a wide range of charting tools and technical indicators to analyze price movements effectively.

User-Friendly Interface: A platform with an intuitive interface will make it easier to navigate and execute trades, especially for beginners.

Robust Security Features: Security is paramount in trading. Choose platforms that offer features like two-factor authentication (2FA) and encryption to protect your account.

OPENING AN ACCOUNT:

Opening a trading account involves several steps, including providing personal information and verification documents. Here's what you need to know:

Personal Information:

Required Details: Be prepared to provide basic personal information such as your full name, date of birth, address, email, and phone number. This information is necessary for account registration and compliance with regulatory requirements.

Verification Documents:

Identification: Most brokers will require a government-issued ID such as a passport or driver's license to verify your identity.

Proof of Address: You will also need to provide proof of address, which can be a recent utility bill, bank statement, or any official document showing your name and address.

Additional Verification: Some brokers may request additional documents or information to comply with anti-money laundering (AML) regulations.

Account Types:

Standard Account: This is the most common type of trading account, suitable for most traders. It allows you to trade with real money and access all the features of the trading platform.

Margin Account: A margin account lets you trade with borrowed funds, increasing your potential profit (and risk). Ensure you understand the risks associated with leveraged trading before opting for a margin account.

Demo Account: A demo account is a great way to practice trading without financial risk. It allows you to trade with virtual money and get familiar with the platform and trading strategies.

FUNDING YOUR ACCOUNT:

Funding your trading account is necessary to start trading. Different brokers offer various funding methods, each with its own advantages.

Deposit Methods:

Bank Transfers: A common and secure method for funding your account. It may take a few days for the funds to appear in your trading account.

Credit/Debit Cards: This method is faster, often instant, but may incur higher fees.

E-Wallets: Services like PayPal, Skrill, and Neteller offer fast and convenient funding options, with lower fees compared to bank transfers and cards.

Minimum Deposit:

Initial Deposit Requirements: Brokers have different minimum deposit requirements. Some may require a significant initial deposit, while others offer lower entry points, making it easier for beginners to start trading.

Currency Options:

Supported Currencies: Check if the platform supports your preferred currency to avoid conversion fees. Some platforms offer multi-currency accounts, allowing you to trade in different currencies without additional costs.

SETTING UP SECURITY MEASURES:

Securing your trading account is critical to protecting your investments and personal information.

Two-Factor Authentication (2FA):

Enabling 2FA: Two-factor authentication adds an extra layer of security by requiring a second form of verification, such as a code sent to your mobile device, in addition to your password. Enable 2FA to enhance your account security.

Secure Passwords:

Password Best Practices: Use strong, unique passwords for your trading account and associated email address. Avoid using easily guessable passwords (like birthdays, anniversaries etc.) and change them regularly (at least once in 90 days).

Regular Monitoring:

Account Monitoring: Regularly monitor your account for any unauthorized activity. Set up alerts for login attempts and account changes to stay informed about any suspicious actions.

Security Updates: Keep your trading platform and any associated software up to date to protect against security vulnerabilities.

By following these steps and taking the necessary precautions, you'll be well-prepared to set up your trading account and begin your journey into gold trading. In the next chapter, we will discuss how to choose the right broker to support your trading activities.

CHAPTER 13: CHOOSING A BROKER

SELECTING THE RIGHT PARTNER FOR YOUR TRADING JOURNEY

Choosing the right broker is critical to your success in gold trading. This chapter will help you identify the key factors to consider when selecting a broker, ensuring you make an informed decision that aligns with your trading needs and goals.

REGULATION AND REPUTATION:

Regulatory Bodies:

Importance of Regulation: A regulated broker is subject to strict rules and oversight by financial authorities, ensuring they operate fairly and transparently. Regulation also provides a level of security and recourse in case of disputes or issues with the broker. You need to confirm that the broker you want to deal with is registered in both its home country and your country of residence.

Key Regulatory Authorities:

Securities and Exchange Commission (SEC) - USA: The SEC regulates brokers in the United States, ensuring compliance with securities laws and protecting investors.

Financial Conduct Authority (FCA) - UK: The FCA oversees brokers in the United Kingdom, ensuring they adhere to high standards of conduct and protecting consumers.

Australian Securities and Investments Commission (ASIC) - Australia: ASIC regulates financial services providers in Australia, ensuring they operate with integrity and fairness.

Broker Reputation:

Research and Reviews: Investigate the broker's reputation by reading online reviews and ratings. Look for feedback from other traders regarding the broker's reliability, transparency, and customer service.

Track Record: Consider the broker's history in the industry. Brokers with a long-standing presence and a solid track record are generally more trustworthy.

TRADING CONDITIONS:

Spreads and Commissions:

Cost Comparison: Compare the spreads (the difference between the bid and ask prices) and commissions charged by different brokers. Higher costs (or spreads) can significantly impact your profitability, especially if you trade frequently.

Fixed vs. Variable Spreads: Some brokers offer fixed spreads, while others offer variable spreads that change based on market conditions. Understand the advantages and disadvantages of each type. Typically, spreads widen when trading volumes are low.

Leverage Options:

Understanding Leverage: Leverage allows you to control a larger position with a smaller amount of capital. While higher leverage can amplify profits, it also increases the risk of substantial losses.

Leverage Limits: Different brokers offer different leverage limits. Ensure the leverage options available align with your risk tolerance and trading strategy.

Execution Speed:

When selecting a broker for your trading activities, prioritizing execution speed is paramount. Efficient order execution ensures that your trades are processed swiftly and at the desired price, minimizing the risk of slippage. Slippage occurs when the actual execution price deviates from the expected price, often due to rapid market movements during order processing.

Key Considerations:

Order Execution Efficiency: Opt for brokers renowned for their ability to execute orders swiftly and accurately. This capability is crucial in fast-moving markets where delays can result in missed opportunities or unexpected losses.

Latency and System Reliability: Assess the broker's trading platform for latency issues and overall reliability, particularly during periods of heightened market volatility. Low latency platforms reduce the time it takes for your orders to reach the market, enhancing your ability to enter and exit trades promptly.

Technology Infrastructure: Understand the broker's technological infrastructure. Brokers with robust systems and high-speed connections to liquidity providers can offer faster order processing times and a smoother trading experience.

Customer Feedback and Reviews: Research customer reviews and feedback regarding the broker's execution speed and reliability. Real-world experiences from other traders can provide insights into how well the broker performs under different market conditions.

CUSTOMER SUPPORT:

Availability:

24/7 Support: Ensure the broker offers customer support that is available when you need it. Ideally, support should be accessible 24/7 to assist you in different time zones and trading hours.

Support Channels:

Multiple Channels: Look for brokers that provide multiple support channels, including live chat, email, and phone support. This ensures you can get help quickly and through your preferred method.

Responsiveness: Test the responsiveness of the broker's customer support. Quick and helpful responses are indicative of good customer service.

Language Support:

Preferred Language: If English is not your first language, check if the broker offers support in your preferred language. Effective communication is crucial for resolving issues and understanding broker policies.

ADDITIONAL SERVICES:

Educational Resources:

Learning Materials: Many brokers provide educational resources such as webinars, tutorials, articles, and e-books. These resources can be invaluable for beginners to learn trading fundamentals and advanced strategies.

Ongoing Education: Look for brokers that offer continuous learning opportunities to keep you updated with the latest market trends and trading techniques.

Demo Accounts:

Practice Trading: A demo account allows you to practice trading with virtual money, giving you the opportunity to test strategies and get comfortable with the platform without financial risk.

Realistic Environment: Ensure the demo account mirrors the live trading environment closely to provide a realistic trading experience.

Research Tools:

Market Analysis: Access to research tools and market analysis can help you make informed trading decisions. Look for brokers that provide daily market updates, technical analysis, and economic calendars.

Proprietary Tools: Some brokers offer proprietary research tools that provide unique insights and data. These can be a valuable addition to your trading toolkit.

By carefully considering these factors, you'll be able to choose a broker that meets your needs and supports your trading journey. In the next chapter, we will discuss understanding trading fees and commissions, another crucial aspect of effective trading.

CHAPTER 14: TRADING FEES AND COMMISSIONS

UNDERSTANDING THE COSTS OF TRADING

Understanding the various fees and commissions associated with gold trading is essential to managing your trading costs and maximizing your profits. This chapter will break down the different types of fees you might encounter, helping you make informed decisions and develop a cost-effective trading strategy.

SPREAD:

The spread is the difference between the bid (buy) and ask (sell) price of gold. It represents the primary cost of trading and is a major way brokers earn money.

Types of Spreads:

Fixed Spreads: Fixed spreads remain constant regardless of market conditions. They offer predictability but might be higher than variable spreads during low volatility.

Variable Spreads: Variable spreads fluctuate based on market volatility. They can be lower than fixed spreads during calm market conditions but may widen significantly during high volatility.

Impact on Trading:

Understanding the type of spread your broker offers and how it fluctuates can help you anticipate trading costs and adjust your strategies accordingly.

COMMISSIONS:

Per Trade Commission:

Some brokers charge a commission per trade in addition to the spread. This fee is typically fixed and is common among brokers offering tighter spreads.

Percentage of Trade Value:

Other brokers may charge a commission based on a percentage of the trade value. This means the larger the trade, the higher the commission.

Comparing Costs:

Compare the overall costs between brokers with different commission structures. A broker with low spreads but high commissions might not always be cheaper than one with higher spreads and no commissions.

SWAP FEES:

If you hold a position overnight, you may incur swap fees (also known as rollover fees). These are charges or credits based on the interest rate differential between the currencies involved in the trade.

Swap fees can add up over time, especially for long-term positions. Check how your broker calculates these fees, which can vary daily, and factor them into your trading strategy.

Strategies to Manage Swap Fees:

When you open and close your trades within the same trading day, you incur no swap fees. Avoiding overnight positions eliminates swap fees altogether.

Consider the interest rate differential when holding positions long-term. This involves understanding the applicable interest rates or swap fees before deciding to trade pairs like XAU/USD, XAU/EUR, or XAU/GBP etc.

DEPOSIT AND WITHDRAWAL FEES:

Funding Fees:

Some brokers charge fees for deposits and withdrawals. These fees can vary depending on the payment method used, such as bank transfers, credit/debit cards, or e-wallets.

Be aware of any minimum withdrawal amounts that might apply and any fees associated with multiple withdrawals. Some brokers might offer a few free withdrawals per month but charge for additional ones.

Manage your funding costs by choosing brokers with low or no deposit/withdrawal fees and ensure your chosen payment method is cost-effective.

INACTIVITY FEES:

Inactivity fees are charged by some brokers if your trading account remains inactive for a specified period.

To avoid inactivity fees, understand the broker's policy regarding inactivity and maintain regular activity in your account, even if it's minimal.

Impact on Long-Term Traders:

If you plan to hold positions for extended periods, choose brokers with no or low inactivity fees to avoid eroding your profits.

MISCELLANEOUS FEES:

Platform Fees:

Some brokers charge fees for using their trading platform or for access to premium features. Ensure you are aware of these costs and whether they provide value for your trading needs.

Currency Conversion Fees:

If you trade in a different currency from your account's base currency, you may incur conversion fees. Understand these costs and how they might impact your overall profitability.

Hidden Costs:

Data Feeds and News Services: Some brokers offer real-time data feeds and news services for a fee. Assess whether these services are necessary for your trading strategy.

Account Maintenance Fees: Check for any ongoing maintenance fees that might apply to your account.

MANAGING TRADING COSTS:

Regularly review your trading statements to understand all the fees being charged. This helps in identifying any unexpected costs and managing your overall trading budget.

Optimizing Trading Strategy:

Incorporate an analysis of trading costs into your strategy development. Choose brokers that align with your trading frequency and style to minimize unnecessary expenses.

By understanding and accounting for these various fees, you can better manage your trading budget and enhance your overall trading strategy.

In the next part, we will delve into advanced trading techniques and strategies to help you refine your skills and maximize your trading success.

PART 5: DEVELOPING A TRADING STRATEGY

CHAPTER 15: SHORT-TERM VS. LONG-TERM TRADING STRATEGIES

In this chapter, we will explore the differences between short-term and long-term trading strategies in the gold market. Understanding these approaches will help you determine which aligns best with your trading goals, risk tolerance, and time commitment.

SHORT-TERM TRADING STRATEGIES:

Day Trading:

Definition: Day trading involves buying and selling gold within the same trading day to capitalize on short-term price movements.

Time Commitment: Requires constant monitoring of the market and quick decision-making to enter a trade. If you are confident of your trade set up (entry, stop loss and take profit levels), you can leave the screen and go do other things.

Tools and Techniques: Utilizes technical analysis, chart patterns, and intraday indicators like moving averages, RSI, and MACD.

Risk and Reward: Offers potential for quick profits but also carries higher risks due to market volatility and rapid price changes.

Scalping:

Scalping is a form of day trading that involves making numerous trades throughout the day to profit from small price movements. Scalp trades can be executed in 1 minute, 3 minutes, 5 minutes, or even 15 minutes time frame.

Time Commitment: Extremely time-intensive, requiring a trader's full attention.

Tools and Techniques: Relies on high-frequency trading tools, tight spreads, and fast execution platforms.

Risk and Reward: High potential for frequent small gains, but significant risk due to transaction costs and market fluctuations.

Swing Trading:

Definition: Swing trading involves holding positions for several days to weeks to capture price swings.

Time Commitment: Less time-intensive than day trading, allowing for market analysis during off-hours.

Tools and Techniques: Combines technical and fundamental analysis to identify trends and reversal patterns.

Risk and Reward: Balances risk and reward by capturing larger price movements than day trading, with lower transaction costs.

LONG-TERM TRADING STRATEGIES:

Position Trading:

Position trading involves holding gold positions for months to years, aiming to profit from long-term trends.

Time Commitment: Minimal daily involvement, with periodic reviews and adjustments.

Tools and Techniques: Heavily relies on fundamental analysis, economic indicators, and long-term trend analysis.

Risk and Reward: Lower risk of short-term volatility but requires patience and the ability to withstand long-term market fluctuations.

Investing:

Investing in gold involves buying and holding physical gold, gold ETFs, or gold mining stocks as part of a diversified portfolio.

Time Commitment: Very low daily involvement, focused on long-term wealth preservation.

Tools and Techniques: Focuses on economic factors, geopolitical events, and monetary policies.

Risk and Reward: Provides a hedge against inflation and economic instability, with potentially lower but steadier returns over time.

CHOOSING THE RIGHT STRATEGY:

Assessing Personal Factors

Risk Tolerance:

Understanding your risk tolerance is crucial for choosing a strategy that you can comfortably stick with, even during market fluctuations.

High Risk Tolerance: If you can handle the stress and potential losses associated with high-risk trades, you might prefer short-term strategies like day trading or scalping, which involve frequent trades and quick decision-making.

Low Risk Tolerance: If you are more risk-averse and prefer steady, less volatile returns, long-term strategies such as investing or position trading might be more suitable. These strategies focus on holding positions for extended periods, reducing the impact of short-term market volatility.

Time Availability:

Consider how much time you can realistically dedicate to trading activities on a daily or weekly basis.

Full-Time Availability: If you have the ability to monitor the markets closely throughout the day, short-term trading strategies like day trading, scalping, or swing trading might fit well. These strategies require constant attention to capitalize on short-term price movements.

Part-Time Availability: If you have a day job and are only available to monitor the markets at specific times, consider short-term trading strategies like swing trading or end-of-day trading. These strategies allow you to analyze the markets and make trading decisions outside of regular work hours, capitalizing on daily or weekly price movements without the need for constant attention.

Limited Time: If you can only dedicate a limited amount of time to trading, long-term strategies that require less frequent monitoring, such as buy-and-hold investing or position trading, may be more appropriate. These strategies involve making fewer trades and focusing on long-term market trends.

Market Knowledge:

Your level of understanding of the gold market and trading tools will influence the complexity of strategies you can effectively employ.

Extensive Knowledge: If you have a deep understanding of market dynamics, technical analysis, and trading platforms, you may be comfortable with complex, short-term strategies that require in-depth market analysis and quick decision-making.

Basic Knowledge: If you are newer to trading or have a more basic understanding of the market, long-term strategies that focus on fundamental analysis might be more appropriate. These strategies allow you to make informed decisions based on broader economic trends and company performance.

BLENDING STRATEGIES:

Hybrid Approach:

Some traders combine short-term and long-term strategies to balance risks and rewards, taking advantage of different market conditions.

Example: A trader might use day trading techniques for immediate opportunities, employ swing trading and position trading to capture medium-term price movements, and hold long-term investments in gold ETFs or mining stocks for stability and long-term growth.

By understanding and choosing the right trading strategy, you can align your trading activities with your personal circumstances, thereby optimizing your chances for success in the gold market. This approach allows you to benefit from the agility of short-term trading while maintaining the security and potential growth of long-term investments.

CHAPTER 16: RISK MANAGEMENT AND DIVERSIFICATION

BUILDING A RESILIENT TRADING PORTFOLIO

Effective risk management and diversification are crucial for protecting your investments and achieving long-term success in gold trading. This chapter will guide you through the principles and techniques of managing risk and diversifying your portfolio.

RISK MANAGEMENT:

A. SETTING STOP-LOSS ORDERS

Stop-loss orders automatically sell or close your position if the price falls to a predetermined level, helping to limit potential losses. Implementing effective stop-loss strategies can protect your capital and provide peace of mind, especially in volatile markets like gold trading.

Implementation:

Technical Support Levels:

Identification: Identify key support levels on your price charts where the price has historically found a floor. These levels are often based on previous lows or areas of significant buying interest.

Setting Stop-Loss: Set your stop-loss order slightly below these support levels. This placement helps to ensure that your position is only sold if the price truly breaks down past a critical point, indicating a potential shift in market sentiment.

Volatility:

Assessment: Assess the current volatility of the gold market. High volatility can cause price fluctuations that might trigger a stop-loss prematurely if it's set too tight.

Adjustment: Adjust your stop-loss levels according to market volatility. In highly volatile conditions, consider setting wider stop-loss limits to prevent your positions from being closed on minor price swings. Conversely, in low-volatility environments, tighter stop-loss orders can help lock in profits without risking too much capital.

Risk Tolerance:

Evaluation: Evaluate your personal risk tolerance. This involves determining the maximum amount of capital you are willing to lose on a single trade without significant stress or impact on your overall trading strategy.

Setting Limits: Set your stop-loss levels to ensure that your potential loss on any single trade does not exceed your predetermined risk threshold, typically 1-2% of your total trading capital. For example, if you have $10,000 in trading capital and a 2% risk tolerance, your maximum loss per trade should not exceed $200.

B. USING TAKE-PROFIT ORDERS:

Take-profit orders automatically sell your position when the price reaches a specified profit level, allowing you to lock in gains without having to constantly monitor the market. Implementing effective take-profit strategies helps maximize profits and maintain trading discipline.

Implementation:

Technical Resistance Levels:

Identification: Identify key resistance levels on your price charts where the price has previously faced difficulty rising above. These levels are often based on previous highs or areas of significant selling interest.

Setting Take-Profit Orders: Set your take-profit orders slightly below these resistance levels. This placement helps to ensure that your position is closed near a potential peak in price, capitalizing on the upward momentum while avoiding the risk of the price reversing before reaching the exact resistance level.

Profit Targets:

Establishment: Establish realistic profit targets based on historical price movements and your overall trading strategy. Analyze past price behavior to understand typical price ranges and potential growth limits.

Consistency with Strategy: Ensure your profit targets are consistent with your risk-reward ratio and overall trading plan. For example, if your stop-loss is set to limit losses to 2% of your trading capital, aim for a profit target that offers at least a 1:2 risk-reward ratio, meaning your take-profit level should capture a 4% gain. This approach helps maintain a balance between potential rewards and the risks involved.

Market Conditions:

Adaptation: Adjust your take-profit levels according to changing market conditions. In a highly bullish market, you might set more ambitious profit targets, while in a volatile or bearish market, more conservative targets might be prudent.

Flexibility: Be flexible and ready to modify your take-profit levels as new information and market dynamics emerge. Regularly review and adjust your targets to align with the current market environment.

Multiple Take-Profit Levels:

Tiered Approach: Consider setting multiple take-profit levels to progressively lock in profits. For example, you could close a portion of your position at an initial target and another portion at a higher target. This tiered approach allows you to benefit from further price increases while securing some gains early.

Position Sizing:

Position sizing involves determining the amount of capital to allocate to each trade based on your risk tolerance and the potential reward.

Implementation:

Position-Sizing Formulas: Use formulas such as the Kelly Criterion or tools that consider your account balance, risk per trade, and potential reward to calculate the optimal trade size.

Risk Percentage: Ensure that each trade does not risk more than a certain percentage of your total capital, commonly 1-2%.

Leverage Management:

Leverage allows you to control a larger position with a smaller amount of capital, amplifying both potential gains and losses.

Implementation:

Cautious Use: Use leverage conservatively to avoid excessive risk. Start with lower leverage ratios and increase gradually as you become more comfortable with the risks.

Margin Requirements: Understand the margin requirements and ensure you have sufficient capital to meet potential margin calls.

DIVERSIFICATION:

Spreading Investments:

Diversification involves spreading your investments across different assets, markets, and instruments to reduce risk.

Implementation:

Mix of Gold Products: Invest in various gold-related products such as physical gold, gold ETFs, gold mining stocks, and futures contracts.

Other Commodities and Asset Classes: Balance your portfolio with other commodities (silver, platinum) and asset classes (stocks, bonds, real estate) to reduce overall risk.

Geographic Diversification:

Geographic diversification reduces risk by spreading investments across different regions and markets.

Implementation:

Regional Investments: Invest in gold markets across different regions, such as North America, Europe, and Asia, to mitigate risks associated with any single market.

Local Political and Economic Factors: Consider the political and economic stability of the regions where you invest.

Sector Diversification:

Sector diversification reduces risk by spreading investments across different industries and sectors.

Implementation:

Various Sectors: Include investments in sectors like technology, healthcare, energy, and consumer goods along with gold mining stocks to balance your portfolio.

Sector Analysis: Regularly analyze the performance and outlook of various sectors to adjust your diversification strategy accordingly.

Periodic Review and Rebalancing:

Regularly reviewing and rebalancing your portfolio ensures that it remains aligned with your risk tolerance and investment goals.

Implementation:

Scheduled Reviews: Conduct reviews quarterly or annually to evaluate the performance of your investments.

Rebalancing: Adjust your portfolio based on performance, market conditions, and any changes in your risk tolerance or investment goals. This may involve selling overperforming assets and buying underperforming ones to maintain your desired allocation.

By mastering risk management and diversification techniques, you can protect your capital and enhance your chances of achieving long-term success in gold trading. In the next chapter, we will discuss setting goals and limits to further refine your trading strategy.

CHAPTER 17: SETTING GOALS AND LIMITS

ESTABLISHING CLEAR OBJECTIVES AND BOUNDARIES FOR TRADING SUCCESS

Setting clear goals and limits is essential for maintaining discipline and achieving long-term success in gold trading. This chapter will help you define your trading objectives, establish limits, and develop a plan to reach your goals.

DEFINING TRADING GOALS:

Short-Term Goals:

Short-term goals are specific, achievable objectives to be accomplished within days, weeks, or months.

Examples:

- Achieving a certain percentage of profit each month.
- Improving technical analysis skills.
- Mastering a specific trading strategy.

Implementation: Break down your goals into actionable steps. For instance, if your goal is to achieve a 5% profit each month, set weekly targets and monitor your progress regularly.

Long-Term Goals:

Long-term goals are broader objectives to be achieved over a year or more.

Examples:

- Building a diversified gold portfolio.
- Reaching a target account balance.
- Achieving financial independence through trading.

Implementation: Develop a roadmap with milestones and timelines. For instance, if your goal is to build a diversified portfolio, outline the steps needed, such as allocating funds to different types of gold investments over a year.

SMART Goals:

SMART goals are Specific, Measurable, Achievable, Relevant, and Time-bound.

Implementation: Use the SMART framework to set clear and actionable trading goals.

Specific: Define clear and precise goals (e.g., "Increase monthly profit by 5%").

Measurable: Ensure your goals can be quantified (e.g., "Achieve a 5% return on investment each month").

Achievable: Set realistic goals based on your skills and market conditions (e.g., "Learn one new trading strategy per quarter").

Relevant: Align goals with your broader financial objectives (e.g., "Expand my trading knowledge to increase long-term profitability").

Time-bound: Set deadlines for achieving your goals (e.g., "Achieve a 5% monthly return within the next six months").

ESTABLISHING LIMITS:

Risk Limits:

Risk limits define the maximum amount of risk you are willing to take on each trade or over a specific period.

Examples:

- Setting a maximum loss limit per trade (e.g., "Risk no more than 2% of total capital on any single trade").
- Implementing a daily loss limit (e.g., "Stop trading for the day if losses exceed 5%").
- Establishing a maximum drawdown percentage for your portfolio (e.g., "Limit total portfolio drawdown to 10%").

Implementation: Use risk management tools and regularly review your risk exposure to ensure compliance with your limits.

Profit Targets:

Profit targets define the level of profit you aim to achieve on each trade or over a specific period.

Examples:

- Setting a profit target per trade (e.g., "Aim for a 3:1 reward-to-risk ratio on each trade").
- Establishing weekly profit targets (e.g., "Achieve a weekly profit of 2% of total capital").
- Setting annual profit goals (e.g., "Increase portfolio value by 20% over the year").

Implementation: Monitor your trades closely and adjust your strategies as needed to meet your profit targets.

Time Limits:

Time limits define the duration you are willing to hold a position or the time you will dedicate to trading activities.

Examples:

- Setting a maximum holding period for trades (e.g., "Hold positions for no longer than two weeks").
- Allocating specific hours for trading each day (e.g., "Trade actively from 9 AM to 12 PM").
- Limiting the time spent on market analysis (e.g., "Spend no more than 2 hours daily on market research").

Implementation: Create a trading schedule and stick to it, ensuring you balance trading with other responsibilities and avoid burnout.

DEVELOPING A TRADING PLAN:

Components of a Trading Plan:

Market Analysis: Define your approach to analyzing the gold market, including the use of technical and fundamental analysis.

Entry and Exit Strategies: Specify the criteria for entering and exiting trades, including the use of indicators, chart patterns, and price levels.

Risk Management: Outline your risk management techniques, including stop-loss orders, position sizing, and leverage management.

Performance Evaluation: Establish a process for regularly reviewing and evaluating your trading performance, identifying areas for improvement.

Sticking to Your Plan:

Discipline: Maintain discipline by following your trading plan consistently and avoiding impulsive decisions.

Flexibility: Be flexible and open to adjusting your plan as market conditions change or as you gain more experience and knowledge.

Implementation: Regularly review and adjust your trading plan to reflect changes in market conditions and your evolving trading skills. Keep detailed records of all trades to analyze performance and refine strategies.

By setting clear goals and limits and developing a comprehensive trading plan, you can navigate the gold market with confidence and work towards achieving long-term success.

In the next part, we will delve into advanced trading techniques and strategies to help you refine your skills and maximize your trading success.

PART 6: TOOLS AND RESOURCES FOR GOLD TRADERS

CHAPTER 18: ESSENTIAL TRADING TOOLS AND SOFTWARE

LEVERAGING TECHNOLOGY FOR ENHANCED TRADING PERFORMANCE

To succeed in gold trading, having the right tools and software is essential. This chapter will explore the various tools and software that can enhance your trading experience and help you make informed decisions.

TRADING PLATFORMS

Desktop Platforms:

MetaTrader 4 (MT4) and MetaTrader 5 (MT5): Widely used platforms known for their comprehensive charting capabilities, extensive range of technical indicators, and automated trading options via Expert Advisors (EAs). They offer robust backtesting tools and are highly customizable to suit different trading strategies.

TradingView: Known for its powerful charting tools and social trading features, TradingView allows traders to share ideas and strategies. It offers a wide range of technical indicators, drawing tools, and the ability to create custom indicators using Pine Script.

Web-Based Platforms:

eToro: Offers a user-friendly interface and social trading features, allowing traders to copy the trades of experienced investors. It provides a wide range of assets, including gold, and features real-time market data and charts.

IG: Provides an advanced web-based platform with comprehensive charting tools, technical indicators, and risk management features. It also offers educational resources and market analysis.

Plus500: Known for its simplicity and ease of use, Plus500 offers real-time market quotes, advanced charting tools, and risk management features, including stop-loss and take-profit orders.

Mobile Apps:

Robinhood: Popular for commission-free trading, Robinhood offers an intuitive mobile app with essential trading features, real-time data, and basic charting tools.

TD Ameritrade Mobile: Provides a comprehensive trading experience with access to real-time data, advanced charting, and educational resources. The app integrates seamlessly with TD Ameritrade's desktop platform.

MetaTrader Mobile: Available for both MT4 and MT5, the mobile app offers full-featured trading, advanced charting tools, and real-time quotes, allowing traders to manage their accounts on the go.

CHARTING TOOLS

Technical Indicators:

Moving Averages: Help smooth out price action to identify trends. Common types include simple moving averages (SMA) and exponential moving averages (EMA).

Relative Strength Index (RSI): Measures the speed and change of price movements, helping to identify overbought or oversold conditions.

Moving Average Convergence Divergence (MACD): Combines moving averages to indicate changes in momentum and trend direction.

Drawing Tools:

Trend Lines: Help identify the direction of the market and potential support and resistance levels.

Fibonacci Retracements: Used to identify potential reversal levels by measuring the extent of price movements.

Support and Resistance Lines: Horizontal lines drawn at levels where the price has historically shown a tendency to reverse direction.

Customizable Charts:

Custom Indicators: Platforms like MT4 and TradingView allow the creation of custom indicators to meet specific trading needs.

Multiple Time Frames: Ability to view charts on different time frames, from minute-by-minute to monthly, providing a comprehensive view of market trends.

Chart Layouts: Save and switch between different chart layouts to analyze multiple strategies and markets.

RISK MANAGEMENT TOOLS

Stop-Loss and Take-Profit Orders:

Stop-Loss Orders: Automatically close a position at a predetermined price to limit losses. Essential for managing risk, particularly in volatile markets.

Take-Profit Orders: Automatically close a position once it reaches a specified profit level, helping to secure gains.

Position Sizing Calculators:

Risk Percentage Model: Determine the appropriate trade size based on a fixed percentage of your account balance at risk per trade.

Fixed Dollar Model: Allocate a fixed dollar amount to each trade, ensuring consistent risk management regardless of market conditions.

Risk-Reward Calculators:

Risk-Reward Ratio: Calculate the potential risk and reward of a trade to ensure it meets your criteria for acceptable risk. Typically, a minimum risk-reward ratio of 1:2 is recommended.

Break-Even Analysis: Determine the price at which a trade will break even, helping to set realistic profit targets and stop-loss levels.

MARKET ANALYSIS TOOLS

Economic Calendars:

Forexfactory.com: Provides a detailed calendar of economic events and releases, along with their potential impact on the markets.

Investing.com: Offers a comprehensive economic calendar with real-time updates on economic indicators, central bank meetings, and geopolitical events.

Tradingeconomics.com: Provides data on economic indicators, forecasts, and historical trends, helping traders analyze macroeconomic factors.

News Aggregators:

Bloomberg.com: Offers real-time financial news, analysis, and market data, covering a wide range of assets, including gold.

Reuters.com: Provides up-to-the-minute news and analysis on global financial markets, commodities, and economic indicators.

Marketwatch.com: Delivers comprehensive market news, analysis, and investment insights, helping traders stay informed about market-moving events.

Sentiment Analysis Tools:

Stocktwits.com: A social platform where traders share market insights and sentiment, helping to gauge market mood and potential trends.

Sentimentrader.com: Offers sentiment analysis tools that track investor sentiment across various markets, providing insights into potential market reversals.

X (Formerly Twitter) and Other Social Media: Monitoring social media platforms for real-time sentiment and news can provide valuable insights into market trends and investor behavior.

By leveraging these essential tools and software, you can enhance your trading experience, make more informed decisions, and improve your overall performance in the gold market.

CHAPTER 19: RELIABLE SOURCES FOR MARKET NEWS AND ANALYSIS

STAYING INFORMED WITH CREDIBLE INSIGHTS AND UPDATES

Staying informed about the latest market news and analysis is crucial for making well-informed trading decisions. This chapter will highlight some of the most reliable sources for market news and analysis, ensuring you have access to accurate and timely information.

FINANCIAL NEWS WEBSITES

BLOOMBERG:

Coverage: Bloomberg offers comprehensive coverage of financial markets, including real-time news, analysis, and data on various assets, including gold. It provides in-depth articles, videos, and market summaries.

Features: Real-time market data, customizable news feeds, economic calendars, and access to Bloomberg TV.

Benefits: Trusted source with extensive global coverage and expert analysis.

REUTERS:

Coverage: Reuters provides in-depth reporting on global financial markets, commodities, and economic indicators. Known for its accuracy and timely reporting.

Features: Real-time news updates, in-depth reports, market data, and analysis tools.

Benefits: A reliable source with a reputation for unbiased reporting and comprehensive coverage.

MARKETWATCH:

Coverage: MarketWatch delivers up-to-date news, market analysis, and investment insights across a wide range of financial assets, including gold.

Features: Real-time news, stock quotes, charts, personal finance advice, and investment tools.

Benefits: Accessible platform with a user-friendly interface and a focus on actionable insights for traders and investors.

GOLD-SPECIFIC NEWS SOURCES

KITCO:

Coverage: Kitco specializes in news and analysis on gold and other precious metals. It offers real-time price updates, expert commentary, and comprehensive market reports.

Features: Live price charts, market commentary, technical analysis, and interviews with industry experts.

Benefits: Focused exclusively on precious metals, providing targeted insights and detailed market information.

GOLDSEEK:

Coverage: GoldSeek provides news, analysis, and forecasts specific to the gold market. It offers a wide range of articles, reports, and expert opinions.

Features: Daily news updates, market analysis, price forecasts, and a community forum.

Benefits: Dedicated to gold, offering deep insights and specialized content for gold traders and investors.

MINING.COM:

Coverage: Mining.com focuses on the mining industry, offering news and analysis on gold mining companies, market trends, and industry developments.

Features: Industry news, company profiles, financial reports, and market analysis.

Benefits: Provides insights into the mining sector, which can impact gold supply and market dynamics.

MARKET ANALYSIS PLATFORMS

TradingView:

Coverage: TradingView offers a social network for traders, featuring user-generated ideas, charts, and analysis across a wide range of financial assets, including gold.

Features: Advanced charting tools, technical indicators, custom scripts, and a community of traders sharing insights.

Benefits: Combines powerful analysis tools with a collaborative community, allowing for the exchange of ideas and strategies.

INVESTING.COM:

Coverage: Investing.com provides a wide range of financial tools, including real-time data, charts, and analysis on gold and other assets. It covers global markets comprehensively.

Features: Economic calendars, technical analysis tools, news updates, and a variety of financial calculators.

Benefits: Extensive resources and tools for both novice and experienced traders, covering a broad spectrum of financial instruments.

SEEKING ALPHA:

Coverage: Seeking Alpha features articles and analysis from a community of investors and traders, covering gold and other financial markets.

Features: Market analysis, investment research, stock ratings, and financial news.

Benefits: Diverse perspectives from a community of contributors, providing a range of insights and investment ideas.

ECONOMIC AND FINANCIAL DATA PROVIDERS

YAHOO FINANCE:

Coverage: Yahoo Finance offers a comprehensive suite of financial data, including gold prices, historical charts, and market analysis.

Features: Real-time market data, financial news, portfolio tracking, and economic indicators.

Benefits: User-friendly platform with extensive financial data and analysis tools.

FRED (Federal Reserve Economic Data):

Coverage: FRED provides access to a vast database of economic data, including indicators relevant to the gold market. It is maintained by the Federal Reserve Bank of St. Louis.

Features: Economic data series, customizable charts, data downloads, and historical trends.

Benefits: Reliable source of macroeconomic data, useful for fundamental analysis and long-term market trends.

TRADING ECONOMICS:

Coverage: Trading Economics offers data on economic indicators, forecasts, and historical trends, helping traders analyze macroeconomic factors.

Features: Economic calendars, country-specific data, and detailed reports on economic indicators.

Benefits: Comprehensive economic data and forecasts, aiding in the analysis of macroeconomic influences on gold prices.

By leveraging these reliable sources for market news and analysis, you can stay informed about market developments, economic indicators, and trends that impact gold prices. This knowledge will enhance your trading decisions and help you navigate the gold market more effectively.

CHAPTER 20: EDUCATIONAL RESOURCES FOR ONGOING LEARNING

EXPANDING YOUR KNOWLEDGE AND ENHANCING YOUR TRADING SKILLS

Continuous learning is vital for staying ahead in the dynamic gold trading market. This chapter will explore various educational resources to help you enhance your trading knowledge and skills.

ONLINE COURSES AND WEBINARS

UDEMY:

Courses Offered: Udemy offers a wide range of courses on trading, technical analysis, and financial markets, including specialized courses on gold trading.

Features: Courses are taught by industry professionals and cover both basic and advanced topics. They include video lectures, quizzes, and downloadable resources.

Examples: "Complete Gold Trading Course," "Technical Analysis Masterclass," and "Day Trading and Swing Trading Strategies."

COURSERA:

Courses Offered: Coursera provides courses from top universities and institutions on trading, economics, and financial analysis.

Features: High-quality courses with structured learning paths, peer-reviewed assignments, and certificates upon completion.

Examples: "Financial Markets" by Yale University, "Trading Strategies in Emerging Markets" by ISB, and "Investment Management" by the University of Geneva.

BROKER-SPONSORED WEBINARS:

IG Academy: Offers free webinars on various trading topics, including technical analysis, risk management, and market updates.

eToro Trading School: Provides webinars on trading basics, platform tutorials, and advanced trading strategies.

TD Ameritrade's Investor Education: Features live and on-demand webinars covering a range of topics, from fundamental analysis to options trading.

BOOKS ON GOLD TRADING AND INVESTMENT

"The New Case for Gold" by James Rickards:

Content: Explores the role of gold in the modern financial system, providing historical context and future predictions. Offers practical insights into gold investment strategies.

Audience: Suitable for both beginners and experienced investors interested in the strategic importance of gold.

"A Complete Guide to the Futures Market" by Jack D. Schwager:

Content: Covers various aspects of futures trading, including gold futures, with practical advice and strategies. It includes detailed explanations of market mechanics and trading techniques.

Audience: Ideal for traders who want to deepen their understanding of futures markets and incorporate gold futures into their trading plans.

"Technical Analysis of the Financial Markets" by John Murphy:

Content: Offers a comprehensive guide to technical analysis, including techniques applicable to gold trading. Covers chart patterns, indicators, and trading strategies.

Audience: Essential reading for traders who use technical analysis to make trading decisions.

ONLINE COMMUNITIES AND FORUMS

Reddit (r/Gold and r/Trading):

Content: Communities where traders and investors share news, analysis, and insights on gold and other markets. Provides a platform for discussing market trends, trading strategies, and current events.

Features: User-generated content, community discussions, and market sentiment analysis.

Elite Trader:

Content: A forum for professional and amateur traders to discuss strategies, tools, and market trends. Includes sections on various asset classes, including gold.

Features: Discussion threads, trading journals, and resource sharing.

Trade2Win:

Content: Provides a platform for traders to share experiences, strategies, and resources across various markets, including gold. Features a diverse community of traders from different backgrounds.

Features: Forums, blogs, trading articles, and educational resources.

PODCASTS AND YOUTUBE CHANNELS

Podcasts:

"The Gold Standard" by Goldmoney: Offers insights into gold markets and economic trends, featuring interviews with experts and discussions on market dynamics.

"Macro Voices": Covers macroeconomic developments that impact gold trading, offering in-depth analysis and expert opinions.

YouTube Channels:

"Bloomberg Markets and Finance": Provides comprehensive market analysis, interviews with industry experts, and up-to-date financial news.

"Trading 212": Features educational videos on trading strategies, market analysis, and tutorials on using trading platforms.

"Rayner Teo": Offers practical trading tips, strategies, and market analysis, focusing on technical analysis and trend following.

By leveraging these tools and resources, you can stay informed, enhance your trading skills, and make more informed decisions in the gold market. In the next part, we will explore advanced trading techniques and strategies to help you refine your skills and maximize your trading success.

PART 7: PRACTICAL TRADING TIPS AND TECHNIQUES

CHAPTER 21: READING GOLD PRICE CHARTS

MASTERING VISUAL TOOLS FOR EFFECTIVE ANALYSIS

Understanding how to read gold price charts is a fundamental skill for any trader. This chapter will guide you through the basics of chart reading, helping you interpret price movements and make informed trading decisions.

TYPES OF PRICE CHARTS

LINE CHARTS:

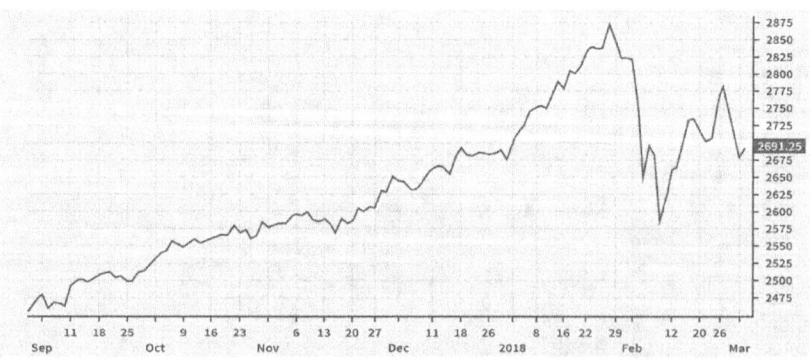

Line Chart: investopedia.com

Line charts are the most basic form of price chart, displaying the closing prices of a financial instrument over a specific time period. Each data point on the chart represents the closing price for a particular day, week, or month, connected by a line.

Advantages:

Simplicity: Line charts are easy to read and provide a clear, uncluttered view of price trends.

Long-Term Perspective: They are ideal for identifying long-term trends and patterns in the market, making them useful for long-term investors.

Clarity: By connecting the closing prices with a continuous line, they offer a straightforward visual representation of price direction, helping traders quickly grasp the overall market sentiment.

Usage:

Trend Analysis: Line charts are best used for gaining a quick overview of price movements and long-term trends. They help traders identify support and resistance levels, trend lines, and potential breakout points.

Simplicity in Decision-Making: For traders who prefer simplicity and clarity, line charts eliminate the noise of intraday price fluctuations, focusing solely on the closing prices.

Historical Data: They are particularly useful for back-testing strategies and analyzing historical price data to understand long-term market behavior.

Example of Use:

When evaluating the long-term performance of a gold investment, a line chart can effectively illustrate the price movements over several years, highlighting major trends, support, and resistance levels without the distraction of intra-day volatility.

BAR CHARTS:

Bar Chart: tradingview.com

Bar charts display the opening, closing, high, and low prices for each trading period. Each bar represents one period of data (e.g., a day, an hour), with the top of the bar showing the highest price, the bottom showing the lowest price, a horizontal line on the left indicating the opening price, and a horizontal line on the right indicating the closing price.

Advantages:

Detailed Information: Bar charts provide more detailed information than line charts, showing the full range of price movement within each period.

Informed Decision-Making: They help traders understand the relationship between the opening and closing prices, as well as the high and low prices, giving a comprehensive view of market activity.

Versatility: Suitable for various trading styles, including day trading, swing trading, and long-term investing.

Usage:

Identifying Price Range and Volatility: Bar charts are useful for identifying the price range (high and low) within specific time periods, helping traders assess market volatility and potential support and resistance levels.

Trend Analysis: They help traders identify trends and patterns, such as uptrends, downtrends, and sideways movements, by comparing the series of bars over time.

Technical Analysis: Bar charts are commonly used in technical analysis to spot chart patterns (e.g., head and shoulders, double tops and bottoms) and to apply various indicators (e.g., moving averages, Bollinger Bands).

Example of Use:

A day trader might use a bar chart to analyze the intraday price action of gold. By examining the high, low, opening, and closing prices for each hour, the trader can identify potential entry and exit points, assess the market's volatility, and make informed decisions based on the observed price behavior.

CANDLESTICK CHARTS:

Candlestick Chart Patterns: moneysukh.com

Candlestick charts are a type of financial chart used to represent price movements over a specific period. Each "candlestick" shows four key pieces of data: the opening price, closing price, high price, and low price for the period. The body of the candlestick represents the range between the opening and closing prices, while the wicks (or shadows) extend to the high and low prices.

Advantages:

Visual Clarity: Candlestick charts provide a more visual and intuitive representation of price action compared to bar charts. The color and shape of the candlesticks make it easier to identify market sentiment and trends at a glance.

- **Color Coding:** Typically, a green (or white) candlestick indicates a period where the closing price was higher than the opening price, signifying bullish sentiment. Conversely, a red (or black) candlestick indicates a period where the closing price was lower than the opening price, signifying bearish sentiment.

Pattern Recognition: Candlestick charts are excellent for identifying specific patterns that can predict future price movements. Common patterns include dojis, hammers, engulfing patterns, and morning/evening stars.

Detailed Information: They provide the same detailed information as bar charts, showing the full range of price movement within each period, but in a more accessible format.

Usage:

Short-Term Analysis: Traders often use candlestick charts for short-term analysis because the visual cues and patterns can help predict immediate price movements. Day traders and swing traders rely on these patterns to make quick trading decisions.

Long-Term Analysis: Candlestick charts are also valuable for long-term analysis. They help investors spot long-term trends and potential reversal points, aiding in strategic decision-making.

Technical Analysis: Candlestick charts are a cornerstone of technical analysis. Traders use them to apply various indicators and oscillators (e.g., RSI, MACD) and to conduct pattern analysis (e.g., identifying head and shoulders, double tops and bottoms).

Example of Use:

A swing trader might use a candlestick chart to analyze daily price movements of gold. By observing the patterns formed by the candlesticks, the trader can identify potential entry and exit points. For instance, if the trader spots a bullish engulfing pattern after a downtrend, it may indicate a potential reversal, prompting the trader to consider entering a long position.

Key Patterns to Watch For:

Doji: Indicates indecision in the market, where the opening and closing prices are virtually the same. This pattern can signal potential reversals, especially when seen after a strong trend.

Hammer and Hanging Man: The hammer appears at the bottom of a downtrend and suggests a potential reversal to the upside. The hanging man appears at the top of an uptrend and suggests a potential reversal to the downside.

Engulfing Patterns: A bullish engulfing pattern forms when a small bearish candlestick is followed by a larger bullish candlestick, suggesting a potential reversal to the upside. Conversely, a bearish engulfing pattern indicates a potential reversal to the downside.

KEY CHART ELEMENTS

Time Frames:

The duration of time that each data point on a chart represents, ranging from 1-minute intervals to monthly intervals.

Considerations: Choose time frames that align with your trading strategy. For instance, day traders might use 1-minute or 5-minute charts, while swing traders might prefer daily or weekly charts.

Price Scale:

Linear Scale: Each unit of price movement is the same distance apart.

Logarithmic Scale: Each unit of price movement is proportional to the percentage change. Useful for analyzing long-term trends where price movements span several magnitudes.

Volume:

The number of shares or contracts traded within a given period.

Importance: High volume often confirms the strength of a price movement, indicating genuine interest from traders and investors.

By mastering these chart-reading skills, indicators and tools, you can better interpret gold price movements, identify trading opportunities, and enhance your overall trading strategy.

CHAPTER 22: IDENTIFYING TRADING SIGNALS AND TRENDS

TECHNIQUES FOR SPOTTING MARKET OPPORTUNITIES

Identifying trading signals and trends is crucial for timing your trades effectively. This chapter will cover the methods and tools used to detect signals and trends in the gold market.

TREND ANALYSIS

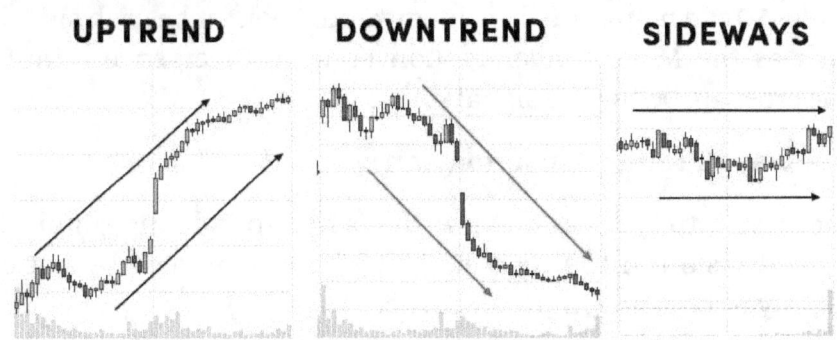

Trend Trading: danielsash.medium.com

Identifying Trends:

Uptrend

Characteristics: An uptrend is identified by a series of higher highs and higher lows, indicating a prevailing positive sentiment and strong buying interest.

Confirmation: Look for consistent upward movements and rising volume. Increased volume during price increases signifies strong buying interest and solidifies the trend's strength.

Indicators: Use moving averages (e.g., 50-day or 200-day) sloping upwards to confirm the trend. Technical indicators like the Relative Strength Index (RSI) above 50 can also support the presence of an uptrend.

Downtrend:

Characteristics: A downtrend is characterized by lower highs and lower lows, signifying a prevailing negative sentiment and selling pressure.

Confirmation: Confirm the downtrend with declining volume and consistent downward movements. Increased volume during price declines indicates strong selling pressure.

Indicators: Moving averages sloping downwards and RSI values below 50 can help confirm a downtrend. Look for bearish signals such as the Moving Average Convergence Divergence (MACD) line crossing below the signal line.

Sideways Trend (Consolidation):

Characteristics: Prices move within a horizontal range, indicating indecision in the market. This phase is marked by flat or slightly fluctuating highs and lows.

Identification: Sideways trends are typically identified through price action moving within a well-defined support and resistance level.

Volume: Volume tends to decrease during consolidation phases as the market lacks a clear direction.

Indicators: Bollinger Bands can be useful to identify consolidation phases. When the bands narrow, it signifies reduced volatility and potential consolidation. The Average Directional Index (ADX) below 20 also indicates a weak trend, suggesting sideways movement.

Trend Strength:

Average Directional Index (ADX): Measures the strength of a trend on a scale from 0 to 100. A reading above 25 indicates a strong trend, while below 20 suggests a weak or nonexistent trend.

Volume: High volume during an uptrend or downtrend confirms the strength of the trend. Low volume suggests a lack of conviction and potential reversal.

TRADING SIGNALS

A. BREAKOUTS:

Breakouts occur when the price moves above a resistance level or below a support level, signaling the potential start of a new trend.

Confirmation: Use volume to confirm breakouts. A breakout accompanied by high volume is more likely to be sustainable.

Application: Identify key support and resistance levels using historical price data. Monitor volume closely to ensure the breakout is genuine and not a false signal.

REVERSALS:

Head and Shoulders:

Pattern: Indicates a reversal of an uptrend. A head and shoulders top is formed by a higher peak (head) between two lower peaks (shoulders).

Signal: A neckline break after the formation of the right shoulder confirms the reversal.

Application: Place a stop-loss above the right shoulder and set profit targets based on the height of the head from the neckline.

Double Tops/Bottoms:

Pattern: Double tops indicate a bearish reversal, forming two peaks at roughly the same level. Double bottoms indicate a bullish reversal, forming two troughs at the same level.

Signal: A break below the trough between the two tops or above the peak between the two bottoms confirms the reversal.

Application: Place stop-loss orders just above the peaks (for double tops) or below the troughs (for double bottoms). Set profit targets based on the distance between the peaks and the trough or vice versa.

CONTINUATION PATTERNS:

Flags and Pennants:

Pattern: Suggest the trend will continue after a brief consolidation. Flags are small rectangular patterns that slope against the prevailing trend. Pennants are small symmetrical triangles.

Signal: The breakout from the flag or pennant indicates the continuation of the trend.

Application: Identify the flagpole (the preceding trend) and project its length from the breakout point to set profit targets.

Triangles:

Ascending Triangles: Suggest a continuation of an uptrend, characterized by a horizontal resistance line and an upward-sloping support line.

Descending Triangles: Suggest a continuation of a downtrend, characterized by a horizontal support line and a downward-sloping resistance line.

Symmetrical Triangles: Can break out in either direction, formed by converging trendlines with no clear horizontal line.

Signal: The breakout direction from the triangle confirms the continuation of the trend.

Application: Use the height of the triangle at its widest point to set profit targets from the breakout point. Place stop-loss orders just outside the opposite side of the triangle.

INDICATORS AND OSCILLATORS

Moving Averages:

Simple Moving Average (SMA): Smooths out price data to identify the direction of the trend.

Exponential Moving Average (EMA): Gives more weight to recent prices, making it more responsive to new information.

Crossovers: A bullish signal occurs when a short-term MA crosses above a long-term MA. A bearish signal occurs when a short-term MA crosses below a long-term MA.

Relative Strength Index (RSI):

Overbought/Oversold: RSI above 70 indicates overbought conditions, suggesting a potential sell signal. RSI below 30 indicates oversold conditions, suggesting a potential buy signal.

Divergence: Occurs when the price makes a new high or low but the RSI does not, indicating a potential reversal.

Moving Average Convergence Divergence (MACD):

Signal Line Crossover:

The MACD consists of two lines: the MACD line and the signal line. The MACD line is derived from the difference between two exponential moving averages (typically the 12-day and 26-day EMAs), while the signal line is a 9-day EMA of the MACD line.

Bullish Signal: A bullish signal occurs when the MACD line crosses above the signal line. This indicates that the short-term moving average is rising faster than the long-term moving average, suggesting upward momentum.

Bearish Signal: A bearish signal occurs when the MACD line crosses below the signal line. This suggests downward momentum as the short-term moving average is falling faster than the long-term moving average.

Application: Traders can use these crossovers to identify potential buy or sell opportunities. For example, a bullish crossover might be a signal to enter a long position, while a bearish crossover might indicate an opportunity to short the asset.

Divergence:

Divergence occurs when the direction of the MACD line diverges from the direction of the price movement.

Bullish Divergence: This occurs when the price makes lower lows, but the MACD line forms higher lows. It suggests that the downward momentum is weakening, and a bullish reversal might be imminent.

Bearish Divergence: This occurs when the price makes higher highs, but the MACD line forms lower highs. It indicates weakening upward momentum and a potential bearish reversal.

Application: Traders can look for divergence as a signal of potential trend reversals. Confirming divergence with other indicators or chart patterns can improve the reliability of these signals.

Bollinger Bands

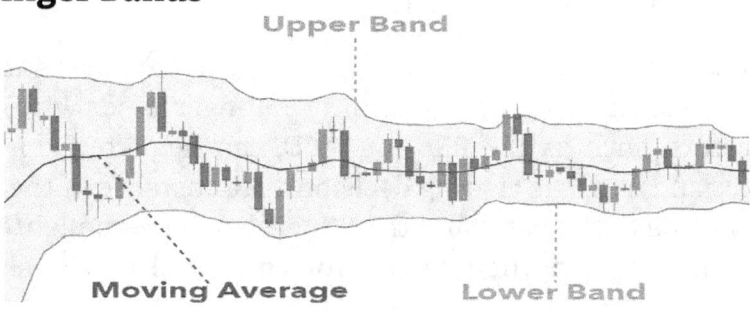

Bollinger Bands: dailyfx.com

Volatility Indicator:

Bollinger Bands consist of three lines: the middle band (a simple moving average), the upper band, and the lower band. The upper and lower bands are typically set two standard deviations away from the middle band.

Widening Bands: The bands widen during periods of high volatility as the standard deviation increases. This expansion indicates that the price is experiencing greater fluctuations.

Contracting Bands: The bands contract during periods of low volatility as the standard deviation decreases. This contraction suggests that the price is stable and experiencing less fluctuation.

Application: Traders can use the width of the Bollinger Bands to gauge market volatility. For example, a sudden expansion in the bands might signal an impending breakout, while contraction might indicate a period of consolidation.

Reversal Points:

Overbought Condition: When the price touches or exceeds the upper Bollinger Band, it may indicate that the asset is overbought and could be due for a pullback.

Oversold Condition: When the price touches or falls below the lower Bollinger Band, it may suggest that the asset is oversold and could be due for a rebound.

Application: Traders can use the Bollinger Bands to identify potential reversal points. Combining Bollinger Bands with other indicators, such as the RSI or MACD, can help confirm these signals and improve trading decisions. For instance, if the price touches the upper band and the RSI is also in overbought territory, it might strengthen the case for a potential sell signal.

COMBINING SIGNALS

Multiple Indicators:

Confirmation: Use a combination of indicators to confirm signals. For instance, a bullish MACD crossover combined with an RSI showing oversold conditions can provide a stronger buy signal.

Avoid False Signals: Relying on a single indicator can result in false signals. Combining multiple indicators reduces the likelihood of errors.

Confluence:

Occurs when multiple signals converge, increasing the reliability of the trading signal.

Examples: A support level coinciding with an RSI oversold condition and a bullish candlestick pattern provides a strong buy signal. Similarly, a resistance level aligning with an overbought RSI and a bearish reversal pattern provides a strong sell signal.

By mastering these methods and tools for identifying trading signals and trends, you can improve your timing and decision-making in the gold market, enhancing your overall trading performance.

CHAPTER 23: COMMON MISTAKES AND HOW TO AVOID THEM

Even experienced traders can make mistakes. This chapter will highlight common mistakes in gold trading and provide tips on how to avoid them.

OVERTRADING

Overtrading involves making too many trades in a short period, often driven by emotional reactions or a lack of a clear strategy.

Avoidance:

Stick to Your Trading Plan: Develop a detailed trading plan with clear entry and exit criteria. Adhere to this plan rigorously to avoid impulsive trades.

Set Limits: Establish daily or weekly trade limits to prevent excessive trading. This helps maintain focus and discipline.

Avoid Emotional Trading: Recognize when emotions like fear or greed are driving your decisions. Take breaks and reassess your strategy to regain objectivity.

IGNORING RISK MANAGEMENT

Failing to implement proper risk management practices, such as setting stop-loss orders, taking on excessive leverage, or risking too much capital on a single trade.

Avoidance:

Use Stop-Loss Orders: Always set stop-loss orders to limit potential losses on each trade. This helps protect your capital from significant downturns.

Manage Leverage: Use leverage cautiously. High leverage can amplify both gains and losses, so ensure it's within your risk tolerance.

Risk Small Percentages: Never risk more than 1-2% of your trading capital on any single trade. This helps preserve your overall capital and allows for recovery from losses.

LACK OF RESEARCH AND PREPARATION

Entering trades without proper analysis or understanding of the market conditions.

Avoidance:

Conduct Thorough Research: Stay updated with the latest market news, economic indicators, and geopolitical events that can impact gold prices.

Perform Technical and Fundamental Analysis: Use both technical analysis (charts, indicators) and fundamental analysis (economic reports, financial news) to inform your trading decisions.

Plan Ahead: Develop a comprehensive trading plan that includes detailed research and preparation before entering any trade.

CHASING LOSSES

Trying to recover losses by making increasingly risky trades, often leading to further losses.

Avoidance:

Accept Losses: Understand that losses are a natural part of trading. Accept them calmly and move on without letting them affect your judgment.

Stick to Your Risk Management Plan: Adhere to your predefined risk management strategies, even after a loss. Avoid making hasty decisions to recover quickly.

Avoid Revenge Trading: Refrain from making trades out of frustration or a desire to get back at the market. Take a break if necessary to clear your mind.

FAILING TO ADAPT

Sticking rigidly to a strategy or plan even when market conditions change.

Avoidance:

Be Flexible: Stay open to adjusting your strategies based on new information or changing market conditions. Be prepared to modify your approach as needed.

Monitor Market Conditions: Continuously monitor the market and be aware of shifts that might affect your trading strategy. Adapt to these changes proactively.

Regularly Review and Update Your Plan: Periodically review your trading plan and strategies. Make necessary adjustments to stay aligned with current market conditions and your evolving trading goals.

By understanding these common pitfalls and how to avoid them, you can enhance your trading performance and work towards achieving consistent success in the gold market. Remaining disciplined, prepared, and adaptable are key to navigating the complexities of gold trading and minimizing potential errors.

PART 8: ADVANCED GOLD TRADING STRATEGIES

CHAPTER 24: OPTIONS AND FUTURES CONTRACTS

ADVANCED STRATEGIES FOR RISK MANAGEMENT AND SPECULATION IN GOLD TRADING

Options and futures contracts are advanced financial instruments that provide gold traders with unique opportunities to manage risk and speculate on price movements. Understanding the mechanics of these derivatives allows you to integrate them into your trading strategy as you build experience and confidence. This integration can greatly enhance your ability to navigate the gold market effectively and improve your trading outcomes.

OPTIONS CONTRACTS

Options contracts provide the holder with the right, but not the obligation, to buy (call option) or sell (put option) gold at a predetermined price (strike price) within a specified period. These contracts are traded on exchanges and offer flexibility in managing risk and generating profits.

Types of Options:

Call Options: These give traders the right (but not the obligation) to buy gold at a specific price (strike price) in the future.

Traders use call options when they believe the price of gold will go up.

Example: Suppose you buy a call option for gold with a strike price of $1800 per ounce and an expiration date in three months. If the price of gold rises above $1800 during this period, you can exercise your option to buy gold at $1800, even if the market price is higher.

Put Options: These give traders the right (but not the obligation) to sell gold at a specific price (strike price) in the future. Put options are used when traders anticipate that the price of gold will decrease.

Example: Let's say you purchase a put option for gold with a strike price of $1700 per ounce and an expiration date in six months. If the price of gold falls below $1700 during this period, you can exercise your option to sell gold at $1700, even if the market price is lower.

Options provide traders with flexibility to profit from both rising and falling gold prices without owning the underlying asset outright. They are valuable tools for managing risk and speculating on future price movements in the gold market.

Benefits:

Leverage: Options contracts offer significant leverage, allowing traders to control a large amount of gold with a relatively small investment. This amplifies potential returns.

Limited Risk: The maximum loss for option buyers is limited to the premium paid for the option, providing downside protection in volatile markets.

Risks:

Premium Decay in Options: When you buy or sell options, the price you pay or receive is called the "premium." Premium decay refers to the gradual reduction in the value of an options contract over time, particularly as it approaches its expiration date. This decay is also known as "theta decay."

Example:

Imagine you buy a call option for gold with a strike price of $1800 per ounce and an expiration date in three months. You pay a premium of $100 for this option.

Scenario 1: Price Increase: If the price of gold rises significantly above $1800 before expiration, the value of your call option could increase due to the potential profit from buying gold at $1800 and selling it at the higher market price.

Scenario 2: Price Stagnation: However, if the price of gold remains close to $1800 or moves very little over the next few months, the value of your call option may decrease gradually. This is because the likelihood of the option being profitable decreases as time passes without the gold price moving above $1800.

Premium decay affects options holders because the longer the time until expiration and the less movement in the underlying asset's price, the more the option's value can erode. Therefore, it's essential for options traders to consider both the direction of the underlying asset's price and the impact of time decay when making trading decisions.

Complexity:

Options trading involves understanding various factors such as options pricing models, implied volatility, and the interplay between different options contracts, making it complex for novice traders.

Strategies:

Covered Calls: Imagine you own gold bars and believe the price won't rise much in the short term. You can sell a "call" option to someone else. This gives them the right to buy your gold at a set price (let's say $2000 per ounce) by a certain date. In return, you get a payment (premium) from them upfront.

If the gold price stays below $2000, the buyer won't use the option, and you keep the premium. If gold rises above $2000, you might have to sell it, missing out on potential profit above $2000.

Protective Puts: Now imagine you're worried the gold price could drop, but you want to hold onto it. You could buy a "put" option. This gives you the right to sell your gold at a set price (say $1800 per ounce) by a certain date, even if the market price falls. You pay a premium for this option.

If the gold price falls below $1800, the put option protects you because you can sell at the higher price of $1800.

Straddles and Strangles: If you think the gold price will move a lot but aren't sure which way, you might use a straddle or strangle. A straddle involves buying both a call and a put option at the same strike price and expiration date. A strangle is similar but uses different strike prices.

These strategies profit from big price moves, no matter if gold goes up or down, but they can be more expensive because you're buying two options.

These strategies give you ways to manage risks and potentially profit from movements in the gold market. Each strategy has its own risks and rewards, so it's essential to understand them well before using them in your trading.

FUTURES CONTRACTS

Futures contracts are standardized agreements to buy or sell gold at a predetermined price on a specified future date. These contracts are traded on futures exchanges and are primarily used for speculation or hedging purposes.

Benefits:

Leverage: Futures contracts provide substantial leverage, allowing traders to control large positions with a relatively small margin deposit. This amplifies potential returns but also increases risk.

Hedging: Futures contracts can be utilized to hedge against price fluctuations in physical gold holdings, thereby protecting against adverse market movements.

Risks:

High Leverage Risk: The significant leverage inherent in futures trading magnifies both potential gains and losses. This can lead to substantial losses that exceed the initial margin deposit.

Mark-to-Market: Futures positions are marked to market daily, meaning gains and losses are realized daily. This can impact margin requirements and necessitate additional capital to maintain positions.

Strategies:

Speculation: Imagine you predict that the price of gold will go up in the future. You can trade "futures" contracts, which are agreements to buy or sell gold at a specific price on a future date.

If you think the price will rise, you might buy a futures contract now at a lower price and sell it later at a higher price, making a profit.

Hedging: Suppose you own a gold mining company and worry that gold prices might fall before you can sell your mined gold.

To protect yourself, you can sell futures contracts at today's price.

If the price falls later, you sell your mined gold at the lower market price, but you make up for it because you locked in a higher price with the futures contract.

Spread Trading: Let's say you notice that gold futures contracts for delivery in different months have different prices. You could buy a futures contract for gold delivery in June and sell another contract for delivery in December.

If the price difference between these contracts widens, you profit from the spread (difference) between the two prices.

To effectively diversify trading strategies, manage risk, and seize market opportunities, understanding and utilizing options and futures contracts in gold trading can be invaluable. However, due to their complexities, it's vital for traders to thoroughly grasp these derivatives and use them cautiously to minimize potential risks.

These tools are best suited for experienced traders who have a deep understanding of market dynamics and risk management principles.

CHAPTER 25: HEDGING AND ARBITRAGE TECHNIQUES

STRATEGIES TO MITIGATE RISK AND EXPLOIT MARKET INEFFICIENCIES

Hedging and arbitrage are sophisticated strategies employed by seasoned traders to manage risk and exploit market inefficiencies in gold trading. Understanding these techniques can provide valuable tools for mitigating losses and maximizing profits. Let's delve deeper into each:

HEDGING

Hedging is like buying insurance to protect yourself from financial losses if things don't go as planned. In gold trading, it means making another trade that goes in the opposite direction of your main trade to reduce the risk of losing money if gold prices change unexpectedly.

Example: Imagine you own a gold mining company and worry that the price of gold might drop. To protect yourself, you could sell gold futures contracts, which would give you the right to sell gold at a fixed price later. If the price of gold falls, you won't lose as much money because you've locked in a higher selling price.

Benefits:

Risk Reduction: By hedging, traders can protect themselves against unfavorable price movements in their gold holdings, ensuring a more stable investment outcome.

Flexibility: Various instruments, including futures contracts, options, and even inverse ETFs, offer flexibility in implementing hedging strategies tailored to specific risk profiles and market conditions.

Techniques:

Using Futures Contracts: One common hedging technique involves entering into futures contracts that lock in the price of gold, thereby safeguarding against future price declines. For example, a gold mining company may sell futures contracts to lock in a selling price for its future production.

Options Hedging: Options provide another avenue for hedging. Traders can purchase put options to hedge against downside risk in their gold holdings. Alternatively, selling covered calls on existing gold positions can generate income and partially offset potential losses.

Diversification: Beyond derivatives, diversifying into other asset classes such as currencies, bonds, or even equities can serve as a hedge against gold price fluctuations. This diversification can reduce overall portfolio risk.

Implementation:

Identify Exposure: Assess the extent of exposure to gold price fluctuations in your portfolio or investment strategy.

Choose Instruments: Select appropriate hedging instruments based on your risk assessment and market outlook.

Monitor and Adjust: Regularly review and adjust hedging positions in response to changing market conditions to ensure they remain effective.

ARBITRAGE

Arbitrage exploits price discrepancies between different markets or instruments to generate risk-free profits. In gold trading, arbitrage opportunities arise when there are differences in the price of gold between various exchanges or related financial instruments.

Benefits:

Risk-Free Profits: Arbitrage seeks to capitalize on price inefficiencies in the market, providing an opportunity for risk-free profits.

Market Efficiency: Arbitrage activities contribute to market efficiency by quickly eliminating price disparities between different markets or instruments.

Techniques:

Spatial Arbitrage: Spatial arbitrage involves exploiting price differences between different geographical markets or exchanges. Traders may buy gold in one market where it's priced lower and simultaneously sell it in another where it's priced higher, thereby capturing the price differential.

Temporal Arbitrage: Temporal arbitrage capitalizes on price differences over time, such as disparities between spot and futures prices. Traders can exploit these differences by taking advantage of pricing anomalies that occur due to factors like supply-demand dynamics or interest rate differentials.

Inter-Market Arbitrage: Inter-market arbitrage involves profiting from price differences between related markets or instruments. For example, traders may exploit pricing inconsistencies between gold futures contracts and related ETFs or mining stocks.

Implementation:

Identify Opportunities: Continuously monitor markets for price discrepancies and arbitrage opportunities using advanced trading tools and algorithms.

Execute Quickly: Given that arbitrage opportunities are often short-lived, swift execution is crucial to capitalize on price differentials before they disappear.

Manage Costs: Consider transaction costs, including commissions and fees, when evaluating arbitrage opportunities to ensure profitability.

By mastering these advanced hedging and arbitrage techniques, traders can enhance their gold trading strategies and achieve better risk-adjusted returns. However, it's essential to remember that these strategies require a deep understanding of market dynamics and risk management principles. Continuous learning, practice, and disciplined execution are key to success in implementing these sophisticated trading techniques.

PART 9: LEGAL AND TAX CONSIDERATIONS

CHAPTER 26: TAX IMPLICATIONS OF GOLD TRADING

ESSENTIAL TAX CONSIDERATIONS FOR SUCCESSFUL GOLD TRADERS

Understanding how taxes affect your gold trading activities is crucial for managing your finances effectively. Here's a detailed look at the key tax implications and strategies to optimize your trading:

INCOME TAX:

Income from gold trading, such as profits from trades, interest from margin accounts, and dividends from gold-related investments, is subject to income tax. The tax treatment depends on whether you're classified as an investor or trader for tax purposes. Investors pay taxes based on their income tax rates, while traders may qualify for tax deductions and concessions.

TAX REPORTING REQUIREMENTS:

Gold traders must accurately report all trading income, capital gains, losses, and other financial transactions to tax authorities. This includes keeping thorough records of trades and investments. Failing to meet reporting requirements can lead to penalties and legal issues.

TAX-EFFICIENT STRATEGIES:

To minimize taxes and maximize profits, consider strategies like timing trades strategically, harvesting tax losses, using retirement accounts, and structuring trades for optimal tax outcomes. Collaborating with tax professionals can help tailor strategies to your specific situation.

INTERNATIONAL TAX CONSIDERATIONS:

If you trade gold internationally, navigate local tax laws, double taxation treaties, withholding taxes, and foreign exchange gains or losses. Tax laws vary by country and can impact your trading decisions significantly. Seek advice from tax experts to manage international tax complexities effectively.

By understanding these tax implications and implementing tax-efficient strategies, gold traders can enhance profitability while ensuring compliance with tax laws. This proactive approach not only reduces tax burdens but also safeguards financial integrity and minimizes risks associated with tax-related penalties.

CHAPTER 27: RECORD-KEEPING BEST PRACTICES

EFFICIENT STRATEGIES FOR ORGANIZING AND MAINTAINING TRADE RECORDS

Maintaining accurate and comprehensive records is essential for gold traders to meet regulatory requirements, facilitate tax compliance, and track trading performance effectively. This chapter will outline record-keeping best practices tailored to gold trading activities, including:

TRADE DOCUMENTATION:

Maintain thorough records of all gold trading activities, such as trade confirmations, transaction receipts, order tickets, and account statements, typically accessible through your online trading platform. These documents are essential for creating a clear audit trail of trades and transactions, ensuring compliance with regulations and facilitating dispute resolution when needed.

PORTFOLIO TRACKING:

Maintaining up-to-date records of investment holdings, positions, and portfolio performance metrics. This includes tracking asset allocation, investment returns, realized and unrealized gains/losses, and benchmark comparisons to assess trading performance accurately.

TAX RECORDS:

Organizing and retaining tax-related documents, such as trade summaries, brokerage statements, tax forms (e.g., Form 1099), and correspondence with tax authorities. These records are essential for fulfilling tax reporting obligations, responding to tax audits, and claiming tax deductions or credits.

By adopting these record-keeping practices, gold traders can enhance transparency, and accountability, while also facilitating tax reporting and decision-making processes effectively. These records serve as valuable assets for assessing trading performance, managing risks, and achieving long-term trading objectives.

PART 10: BUILDING AND MANAGING YOUR PORTFOLIO

CHAPTER 28: PORTFOLIO DIVERSIFICATION STRATEGIES

STRATEGIES FOR A BALANCED GOLD INVESTMENT PORTFOLIO

Diversification is not merely a prudent investment strategy; it's a fundamental principle for managing risk and optimizing returns in a portfolio. Gold's unique characteristics make it an essential component of diversified investment portfolios. Let's explore each diversification strategy in more detail:

ASSET CLASS DIVERSIFICATION

By allocating assets across different asset classes, investors can reduce the overall risk of their portfolios. Gold's low correlation with traditional asset classes like equities and bonds makes it an effective diversifier. During times of market turmoil or economic uncertainty, gold often acts as a safe-haven asset, preserving capital when other assets falter. Moreover, gold's ability to retain its value over the long term serves as a hedge against inflation, further enhancing its appeal as a diversification tool.

GEOGRAPHIC DIVERSIFICATION

Investing in gold assets from diverse geographic regions helps mitigate geopolitical risks, currency fluctuations, and regional economic factors. Gold mining companies, for example, operate in various countries, each with its own regulatory environment, political stability, and mining practices. By holding gold assets from different jurisdictions, investors spread their risk and reduce exposure to country-specific events that could adversely affect their investments.

SECTOR DIVERSIFICATION

Within the gold sector itself, there are various sub-sectors that investors can explore to diversify their exposure. These include gold mining companies, royalty/streaming companies, exploration firms, and gold-backed exchange-traded funds (ETFs). Each sub-sector has its own risk-return profile and may perform differently under different market conditions. By diversifying across these sub-sectors, investors can reduce company-specific risks and sector-specific volatility while maintaining exposure to the underlying commodity.

TIME HORIZON DIVERSIFICATION

Investors should tailor their allocation to gold based on their investment horizon and risk tolerance. Long-term investors seeking wealth preservation and protection against inflation may allocate a significant portion of their portfolio to gold as a strategic asset. In contrast, short-term traders may use gold for tactical portfolio adjustments, taking advantage of short-term price fluctuations or hedging against near-term market risks.

PORTFOLIO REBALANCING

Regularly reviewing and rebalancing a portfolio is essential for maintaining target asset allocations and optimizing risk-adjusted returns. As asset values fluctuate over time, the original asset allocation may deviate from the desired targets. Rebalancing involves selling assets that have appreciated and buying assets that are undervalued to realign the portfolio with its target allocation. This disciplined approach ensures that investors stay true to their investment objectives and risk tolerance levels over time.

By incorporating these diversification strategies into their investment approach, investors can build more resilient portfolios that are better positioned to weather market volatility and achieve their long-term financial goals. Gold's role as a diversifier adds value by reducing portfolio risk and enhancing overall returns, making it a valuable asset for investors seeking to build wealth over time.

CHAPTER 29: INVESTING IN GOLD AND GOLD ASSETS

MAXIMIZING RETURNS THROUGH DIVERSIFIED GOLD INVESTMENTS

Investing in gold and related assets is a cornerstone strategy for many investors looking to diversify their portfolios, hedge against inflation, and secure their wealth. This chapter will guide you through various methods of investing in gold, from physical gold to financial instruments tied to gold prices, helping you make informed decisions based on your investment goals, risk tolerance, and market conditions.

1. PHYSICAL GOLD

BULLION AND COINS

Physical gold includes bullion bars and coins, which can be bought from dealers, banks, or mints. This form of gold investment allows you to own a tangible asset that holds intrinsic value.

Advantages:

Tangible Asset: You own a physical item that you can store and use as a hedge against economic instability. This can provide peace of mind during periods of financial uncertainty.

No Counterparty Risk: Unlike financial instruments, physical gold carries no default risk, meaning its value isn't dependent on a company's performance or solvency.

Disadvantages:

Storage and Insurance Costs: Secure storage and insurance are necessary to protect your investment. These additional costs can reduce overall returns.

Liquidity: Selling physical gold can sometimes be less liquid and involve higher transaction costs compared to financial instruments. Finding a buyer and agreeing on a price can take time.

How to Profit:

Buy Low, Sell High: Purchase gold bullion and coins when prices are low and sell when prices increase. Monitoring market trends and economic indicators can help you make informed decisions.

Hedge Against Inflation: Use physical gold as a hedge against inflation. As currency values decrease, the price of gold typically rises, preserving your purchasing power.

Diversify Portfolio: Add gold bullion and coins to diversify your investment portfolio. This can reduce overall risk and enhance returns, especially during market downturns.

Leverage Premiums: Some coins carry numismatic value, meaning they are worth more than their weight in gold due to rarity or historical significance. Investing in these can lead to higher profits if demand increases.

JEWELRY

Gold jewelry can also serve as an investment, though it's typically purchased for personal enjoyment. This form of gold investment combines aesthetic appeal with financial value.

Advantages:

Dual Purpose: Combines aesthetic value with investment potential. You can enjoy wearing the jewelry while also holding a valuable asset.

Personal Enjoyment: Jewelry allows you to showcase your wealth and personal style. It can also hold sentimental value, making it a cherished possession.

Disadvantages:

High Premiums: The craftsmanship and design often mean paying a premium above the gold content value. This premium can be significant, reducing the immediate investment value.

Wear and Tear: Physical use can diminish value over time. Scratches, dents, and other damage can reduce the resale value of the jewelry.

How to Profit:

Buy Quality Pieces: Invest in high-quality jewelry with high gold content (e.g., 18k or 24k). High gold content retains more value.

Opt for Renowned Brands: Jewelry from renowned designers or brands can hold or even increase in value over time. Brand reputation can significantly impact resale value.

Monitor Gold Prices: Keep an eye on gold market trends. If gold prices rise significantly, you can consider selling your jewelry to capitalize on the increase.

Limited Editions: Investing in limited edition or unique pieces can provide higher returns due to their rarity. These items often appreciate in value over time.

Care and Maintenance: Properly maintain your jewelry to preserve its condition. Regular cleaning and careful storage can prevent wear and tear, maintaining its value.

Sell Strategically: Timing is crucial. Sell your jewelry during periods of high gold prices or when there's high demand for luxury items. Use reputable dealers or auction houses to get the best price.

Example: Imagine you purchase a limited edition gold necklace from a renowned designer. The necklace is made of 18k gold and is part of a collection that's known for its craftsmanship and design. Over the years, as gold prices rise and the necklace remains in excellent condition, its value increases. You decide to sell the necklace during a peak in gold prices, fetching a higher price than what you originally paid, thus making a profit while having enjoyed the piece throughout the years.

2. GOLD ETFS AND MUTUAL FUNDS

Gold ETFs (Exchange-Traded Funds) and mutual funds track the price of gold and are traded on stock exchanges. These financial instruments allow investors to gain exposure to gold prices without physically owning the metal.

Advantages:

Ease of Access: Gold ETFs and mutual funds can be bought and sold like stocks, providing liquidity and ease of transaction. Investors can quickly enter or exit positions during trading hours.

No Storage Issues: Unlike physical gold, gold ETFs and mutual funds do not require secure storage. This eliminates the costs and logistics associated with storing physical gold.

Diversification: Some funds invest in a range of gold-related assets, such as gold mining stocks, offering additional diversification within the gold sector.

Disadvantages:

Management Fees: These funds may include annual management fees that can impact returns. It's essential to consider these fees when calculating potential profits.

Market Risk: Prices can be affected by market sentiment and other factors unrelated to the gold market. Economic events, investor behavior, and broader market trends can influence the price of ETFs and mutual funds.

Tracking Error: Some ETFs may not perfectly track the price of gold due to management strategies or other factors, leading to slight deviations from gold's actual price movements.

How to Profit:

Timing the Market: Buy gold ETFs or mutual funds when you anticipate a rise in gold prices. Monitor market trends, economic indicators, and geopolitical events that could drive gold prices up.

Cost-Averaging Strategy: Regularly invest a fixed amount in gold ETFs or mutual funds regardless of the price. This strategy, known as dollar-cost averaging, can reduce the impact of volatility and lower the average cost per share over time.

Leverage Geopolitical Events: Gold often serves as a safe haven during geopolitical tensions or economic uncertainties. Investing in gold ETFs during such periods can lead to substantial profits as demand for gold rises.

Reinvestment of Dividends: Some gold ETFs and mutual funds pay dividends, which can be reinvested to buy more shares, compounding your returns over time.

Hedging Against Inflation: Use gold ETFs as a hedge against inflation. Gold prices tend to rise when inflation increases, preserving purchasing power and potentially leading to profits.

Short-Term Trading: For experienced traders, capitalizing on short-term price movements through active trading can yield profits. This requires a good understanding of technical analysis and market trends.

Example: Suppose you invest in a gold ETF when the price of gold is $1,200 per ounce, anticipating an increase due to upcoming geopolitical tensions. Over the next few months, the price of gold rises to $1,400 per ounce, driven by increased investor demand for safe-haven assets. You decide to sell your ETF shares, realizing a significant profit from the price appreciation. Additionally, if you had been reinvesting dividends paid by the ETF, your overall returns would be further enhanced.

3. GOLD MINING STOCKS

Investing in shares of gold mining companies means buying a stake in companies that explore, mine, and produce gold. These stocks are traded on major stock exchanges and provide investors with exposure to the gold market through the operational performance of mining firms.

Advantages:

Leverage to Gold Prices: Gold mining stocks often provide greater returns than gold itself during bull markets. This is because the profits of mining companies can increase exponentially with rising gold prices due to operational leverage.

Dividends: Some gold mining companies pay dividends, offering investors a stream of income in addition to potential capital appreciation. This can make mining stocks attractive for income-focused investors.

Growth Potential: Mining companies may discover new gold reserves or improve their extraction processes, leading to increased production and potentially higher stock prices.

Disadvantages:

Company Risk: The performance of gold mining stocks depends on the operational success of the company, which involves risks such as production costs, management decisions, and exploration results. These factors can affect the company's profitability independent of gold prices.

Volatility: Mining stocks can be more volatile than gold prices due to company-specific risks and broader market factors, such as changes in government regulations, environmental policies, and geopolitical stability in mining regions.

Market Risk: Broader stock market trends and investor sentiment can influence the price of mining stocks, leading to fluctuations that do not directly correlate with gold prices.

How to Profit:

Research and Selection: Conduct thorough research to select well-managed gold mining companies with strong balance sheets, efficient operations, and promising growth prospects. Look for companies with proven reserves and a track record of profitable production.

Timing the Market: Invest in mining stocks during periods of anticipated gold price increases. This can amplify your returns as the profitability of mining companies improves with rising gold prices.

Dividend Reinvestment: Reinvest dividends paid by mining companies to buy more shares. This can compound your returns over time, especially if the company consistently increases its dividend payouts.

Diversification: Diversify your investment across multiple mining companies to spread risk. Investing in a mix of large, established miners and smaller, exploration-focused firms can balance the potential for high returns with stability.

Long-Term Growth: Hold mining stocks for the long term to benefit from the discovery of new reserves, technological advancements in mining, and overall growth in the gold market. This approach can lead to substantial capital appreciation over time.

Hedging Against Inflation: Use mining stocks as a hedge

against inflation. As gold prices typically rise with inflation, the increased value of gold can boost the profitability of mining companies, protecting your investment's purchasing power.

Example: Imagine you invest in shares of a gold mining company like Barrick Gold Corporation when the gold price is $1,200 per ounce. Over the next year, due to geopolitical tensions and inflation concerns, the gold price rises to $1,500 per ounce. Barrick Gold, with its efficient operations and low production costs, reports significantly higher profits, leading to a substantial increase in its stock price. Additionally, Barrick Gold pays quarterly dividends, which you reinvest to buy more shares, further increasing your investment's value. By carefully selecting and holding mining stocks, you benefit from both the rising gold prices and the company's operational success.

4. GOLD FUTURES AND OPTIONS

Gold futures and options are derivative contracts that allow investors to speculate on or hedge against future movements in gold prices. Futures contracts obligate the buyer to purchase, and the seller to sell, a specific amount of gold at a predetermined price on a future date. Options contracts give the buyer the right, but not the obligation, to buy (call options) or sell (put options) gold at a specified price within a certain timeframe.

Advantages:

Leverage: Futures and options allow investors to control large amounts of gold with a relatively small initial investment. This means that small price movements can result in significant profits.

Hedging: These instruments are effective tools for managing risk in gold investments. For example, a gold mining company might use futures contracts to lock in the selling price of its future gold production, protecting against price declines.

Flexibility: Options provide flexibility as they offer the right but not the obligation to buy or sell gold, allowing traders to tailor their strategies to different market conditions.

Disadvantages:

Complexity: Trading futures and options requires a deep understanding of derivatives markets, contract specifications, and the factors influencing gold prices. It can be complex and is not recommended for beginners.

Potential for Significant Losses: Leveraged positions can lead to large losses if the market moves against you. Since futures contracts are binding, failure to meet margin calls can result in substantial financial damage.

Expiration Dates: Futures and options contracts have expiration dates, which means that timing is crucial. If the market does not move in your favor within the contract period, you can incur losses.

How to Profit:

Speculation: Traders can profit from correctly predicting the direction of gold prices. For example, if you believe gold prices will rise, you can buy futures contracts or call options. If gold prices do increase, you can sell the contracts at a higher price or exercise the options for a profit.

Hedging: Investors can use futures and options to protect their gold investments from adverse price movements. For instance, a gold jewelry manufacturer might buy put options to guard against potential drops in gold prices, ensuring that they can sell their jewelry at a favorable price.

Spread Trading: Involves taking positions in different contracts to profit from the price differences between them. For example, you might buy a near-term futures contract and sell a long-term futures contract if you believe the price difference between the two will widen.

Example: Imagine you are a gold trader who believes that gold prices, currently at $1,800 per ounce, will rise to $2,000 per ounce in the next three months. You decide to buy a gold futures contract that expires in three months, agreeing to buy 100 ounces of gold at the current price. The contract requires an initial margin of $10,000. If gold prices do rise to $2,000 per ounce, you can sell the contract for $200,000 (100 ounces x $2,000), yielding a profit of $20,000 ($200,000 - $180,000), minus any fees.

5. DIGITAL GOLD

Digital gold involves purchasing gold through online platforms where the gold is stored in secure vaults on behalf of the investor. Examples of such online platforms include BullionVault, GoldMoney, Vaulted, OneGold, Aurum etc. These platforms allow investors to buy, sell, and store gold without having to handle the physical metal themselves..

Advantages:

Convenience: Digital gold platforms make it easy to buy and sell gold with just a few clicks. Investors can transact at any time from anywhere, eliminating the need for physical handling and storage.

Lower Costs: Digital gold often comes with lower premiums and storage costs compared to buying and storing physical gold. This can result in higher net returns for the investor.

Fractional Ownership: Investors can buy gold in small amounts, even fractions of a gram, making it accessible to a wider range of people with varying budgets.

Transparency: Most digital gold platforms provide real-time updates on gold prices and the amount of gold held by the investor, ensuring transparency.

Disadvantages:

Trust and Security: Investors must trust the digital platform and the security of their storage facilities. There is a risk that the platform could be hacked or mismanage the gold holdings.

Regulatory Risks: The digital gold market could be impacted by regulatory changes, which might affect the operation of platforms and the security of investments.

Lack of Physical Access: Investors do not have immediate physical access to their gold, which might be a concern for those who prefer to hold tangible assets.

Counterparty Risk: The reliance on a third-party platform introduces counterparty risk, meaning that the investor's gold is dependent on the platform's solvency and operational integrity.

How to Profit:

Buying Low and Selling High: Like other forms of gold investment, the primary way to profit from digital gold is by buying when prices are low and selling when prices rise. Investors can take advantage of market fluctuations to make profitable trades.

Example: Suppose you purchase digital gold at $1,800 per ounce. If the price rises to $2,000 per ounce, you can sell your holdings and realize a profit of $200 per ounce, minus any transaction fees.

Cost Averaging: By investing a fixed amount of money regularly, regardless of the gold price, you can average out the cost of your gold purchases. This strategy helps mitigate the impact of short-term price volatility.

Example: You decide to invest $100 in digital gold every month. When prices are high, you buy less gold, and when prices are low, you buy more. Over time, this strategy can result in a favorable average purchase price.

Hedging: Digital gold can be used to hedge against economic uncertainty and inflation. Holding digital gold can protect your portfolio's value when other assets, such as stocks or currencies, are underperforming.

Example: During times of economic turmoil or high inflation, you can increase your digital gold holdings to safeguard your investment portfolio. If the value of traditional assets declines, the rise in gold prices can help offset those losses.

Portfolio Diversification: Including digital gold in your investment portfolio can provide diversification benefits. Gold often has a low correlation with other asset classes, such as stocks and bonds, which can reduce overall portfolio risk.

Example: If your portfolio is heavily weighted towards equities, adding digital gold can balance your investments. During a stock market downturn, gold prices might rise, providing a buffer against losses in your equity holdings.

6. GOLD-BACKED CRYPTOCURRENCIES

Gold-backed cryptocurrencies are digital currencies that represent ownership of physical gold stored by a trusted entity. Each unit of the cryptocurrency is typically pegged to a specific amount of gold, combining the stability of gold with the innovative features of cryptocurrencies.

Advantages:

Innovative Investment: These digital currencies offer a modern way to invest in gold, leveraging blockchain technology to provide a new form of asset. They combine the historical stability and value retention of gold with the flexibility and accessibility of cryptocurrencies.

Example: If you purchase 1 unit of a gold-backed cryptocurrency, it might represent 1 gram of gold stored in a secure vault.

This allows you to hold and trade gold easily without needing to handle the physical metal.

Transparency: Many gold-backed cryptocurrency platforms offer real-time verification of their gold reserves. This transparency helps build trust among investors, ensuring that each digital token is indeed backed by the corresponding amount of physical gold.

Example: A platform might provide online access to audit reports or live video feeds of the gold reserves, giving investors confidence in the legitimacy of their holdings.

Lower Transaction Costs: Trading gold-backed cryptocurrencies often incurs lower transaction costs compared to buying, storing, and selling physical gold. This can enhance net returns for investors.

Example: Traditional gold investments may involve significant costs for storage, insurance, and transaction fees, whereas trading gold-backed cryptocurrencies typically involves minimal blockchain transaction fees.

Disadvantages:

Market Risk: While gold itself is relatively stable, the value of gold-backed cryptocurrencies can be subject to the volatility of the broader cryptocurrency market. Regulatory changes, technological advancements, and market sentiment can all impact their prices.

Example: If a major regulatory body imposes restrictions on cryptocurrency trading, the value of gold-backed cryptocurrencies could drop, even if the price of gold remains stable.

Technology Risk: These digital assets rely on the security and reliability of blockchain technology. If the underlying technology is compromised, or if there are issues with the platform's infrastructure, investors could face significant risks.

Example: A hacking incident or a technical glitch on the platform could lead to loss of assets or disruptions in trading.

Regulatory Risks: The regulatory environment for cryptocurrencies is still evolving, and gold-backed cryptocurrencies are not immune to legal and regulatory challenges. Changes in laws or regulations can affect their acceptance and usability.

Example: Governments may introduce new regulations that limit or restrict the use of gold-backed cryptocurrencies, impacting their liquidity and market acceptance.

How to Profit:

Price Appreciation: Investors can profit from the increase in the value of gold-backed cryptocurrencies as the price of gold rises. Since these digital currencies are pegged to physical gold, their value should move in tandem with gold prices.

Example: If you buy a gold-backed cryptocurrency when the price of gold is $1,800 per ounce and sell it when the price rises to $2,000 per ounce, you can profit from the appreciation in value.

Arbitrage Opportunities: Given the nature of cryptocurrencies and global markets, there may be opportunities to profit from price differences in gold-backed cryptocurrencies across different exchanges.

Example: If a gold-backed cryptocurrency is priced lower on one exchange compared to another, you can buy on the cheaper exchange and sell on the more expensive one to profit from the price difference.

Hedging: Gold-backed cryptocurrencies can be used as a hedge against market volatility and economic uncertainty. By holding a stable asset like gold in digital form, investors can protect their portfolios from market downturns.

Example: During a financial crisis or period of high inflation, the value of traditional assets might decline. Holding gold-backed cryptocurrencies can provide a stable store of value, mitigating losses in other parts of your portfolio.

Diversification: Including gold-backed cryptocurrencies in an investment portfolio can offer diversification benefits, reducing overall portfolio risk.

Example: If your investment portfolio is heavily weighted towards equities or fiat currencies, adding gold-backed cryptocurrencies can balance your risk profile and provide a buffer against market fluctuations.

Investing in gold and gold-related assets offers a range of options to suit different investment strategies and risk profiles. Whether you prefer the tangibility of physical gold, the convenience of ETFs, the potential high returns of mining stocks, or the advanced strategies of futures and options, there is a gold investment that can align with your financial goals.

As always, thorough research and a clear understanding of each investment type's risks and benefits are crucial to making informed decisions and achieving long-term success in gold investing.

CHAPTER 30: BALANCING GOLD WITH OTHER INVESTMENTS

STRATEGIES FOR CREATING A DIVERSIFIED PORTFOLIO

Balancing gold with other investments requires careful consideration of various factors, including risk management, correlation analysis, portfolio optimization, and risk-adjusted returns. Let's delve deeper into each of these strategies:

RISK MANAGEMENT

Before determining the allocation to gold in your portfolio, it's essential to assess your risk tolerance, investment objectives, and time horizon. Conservative investors, who prioritize capital preservation and downside protection, may allocate a higher percentage of their portfolio to gold. In contrast, aggressive investors, who seek higher returns and can tolerate greater volatility, may allocate a smaller portion to gold.

CORRELATION ANALYSIS

Conducting correlation analysis helps identify the relationship between gold and other asset classes, such as equities, bonds, and real estate. Gold's negative correlation with equities during market downturns makes it an effective hedge against equity market volatility. By diversifying into assets with low or negative correlations, investors can reduce overall portfolio risk without sacrificing returns.

PORTFOLIO OPTIMIZATION

Modern portfolio theory (MPT) provides a framework for optimizing portfolio allocations based on expected returns, volatilities, and correlations. Asset allocation models, such as mean-variance optimization, help investors construct portfolios that offer the highest level of diversification for a given level of risk. By incorporating gold into a diversified portfolio, investors can achieve more efficient risk-return profiles and potentially enhance long-term performance.

RISK-ADJUSTED RETURNS

Evaluating the risk-adjusted returns of a portfolio is essential for assessing its overall performance. Metrics such as the Sharpe ratio, which measures the excess return per unit of risk, and the Sortino ratio, which focuses on downside risk, provide valuable insights into portfolio efficiency. Incorporating gold into a portfolio can improve risk-adjusted returns by reducing downside risk and enhancing portfolio stability, particularly during periods of market turmoil.

By carefully balancing gold with other investments based on risk management principles, correlation analysis, portfolio optimization techniques, and risk-adjusted return metrics, investors can construct portfolios that are well-diversified, resilient to market fluctuations, and better positioned to achieve their long-term financial goals.

CHAPTER 31: PERIODIC REVIEW AND REBALANCING

MAINTAINING A BALANCED PORTFOLIO THROUGH REGULAR ASSESSMENT

Successful portfolio management requires ongoing monitoring and periodic adjustments to ensure alignment with investment objectives and market conditions. Expanding on the importance of periodic review and rebalancing in portfolio management involves delving into several key aspects:

REVIEW PROCESS

Establishing a systematic review process ensures that investors regularly evaluate their portfolio's performance and alignment with their investment objectives. This process may involve setting predefined intervals, such as quarterly or annually, for portfolio reviews. Additionally, investors may conduct ad-hoc reviews in response to significant market events or changes in their financial circumstances.

PERFORMANCE EVALUATION

During portfolio reviews, investors assess the performance of individual assets, sectors, and the overall portfolio relative to benchmarks and investment goals. This evaluation helps identify underperforming assets and areas for improvement. By analyzing performance metrics such as return on investment, volatility, and correlation, investors can make informed decisions about portfolio adjustments.

REBALANCING STRATEGIES

Portfolio rebalancing involves realigning the portfolio's asset allocation with its target weights. Investors may rebalance their portfolios based on predetermined criteria, such as percentage deviations from target allocations or specific thresholds for asset class weights. Rebalancing typically involves buying or selling assets to restore the desired asset mix. This process helps investors maintain diversification and manage risk effectively.

TAX CONSIDERATIONS

When rebalancing a portfolio, investors must consider the tax implications of their actions. Capital gains taxes may be incurred when selling appreciated assets, potentially impacting overall portfolio returns.

To minimize tax liabilities, investors can implement tax-efficient rebalancing strategies, such as tax-loss harvesting, which involves selling underperforming assets to offset capital gains. Additionally, utilizing tax-advantaged accounts, such as retirement accounts or health savings accounts, can help mitigate the tax impact of portfolio rebalancing.

By implementing a disciplined approach to periodic review and rebalancing, investors can ensure that their portfolios remain aligned with their investment objectives, risk tolerance, and changing market conditions. This proactive approach to portfolio management helps investors navigate market volatility, optimize returns, and achieve long-term financial success.

PART 10: THE FUTURE OF GOLD TRADING

CHAPTER 32: EMERGING TRENDS IN THE GOLD MARKET

In recent years, the gold market has witnessed several emerging trends that are reshaping the landscape of gold trading. Understanding and adapting to these trends are crucial for traders to stay competitive and capitalize on new opportunities. Let's delve deeper into each of these emerging trends:

DIGITAL GOLD

The rise of digital gold platforms, facilitated by blockchain technology, has revolutionized the way investors access and trade gold. These platforms allow investors to buy, sell, and trade fractional ownership of physical gold in a digital format, often backed by physical gold reserves stored in secure vaults.

Digital gold offerings provide investors with greater flexibility, accessibility, and transparency compared to traditional gold investments. As digital gold platforms continue to gain traction, they are likely to play an increasingly significant role in the gold market ecosystem.

SUSTAINABLE AND ETHICAL SOURCING

There is a growing emphasis on sustainable and ethical sourcing practices in the gold industry. Investors are increasingly concerned about the environmental and social impacts of gold mining and production. As a result, there is a growing demand for responsibly sourced gold, mined and produced in accordance with stringent environmental and social standards.

Companies that adhere to sustainable and ethical practices are likely to attract greater investor interest and command a premium in the market. Additionally, regulatory bodies are imposing stricter regulations on gold mining companies to ensure compliance with environmental and social standards.

GOLD-BACKED CRYPTOCURRENCIES

The convergence of gold and cryptocurrencies has led to the emergence of gold-backed digital currencies or stablecoins. These cryptocurrencies are pegged to the value of physical gold, providing investors with a digital representation of the precious metal. Gold-backed cryptocurrencies offer a unique blend of the stability of gold and the flexibility of cryptocurrencies, making them an attractive investment option for individuals seeking exposure to both asset classes.

As the cryptocurrency market continues to mature, gold-backed stablecoins are expected to gain traction among investors looking for a safe haven asset with reduced volatility.

CENTRAL BANK POLICIES

Central banks play a pivotal role in influencing the gold market through their monetary policies and gold reserve management. In recent years, there has been a trend among central banks to increase their gold reserves as a strategic asset allocation. Central banks view gold as a hedge against currency devaluation, inflation, and geopolitical risks.

As a result, they have been actively accumulating gold reserves to diversify their foreign exchange reserves and reduce their reliance on traditional reserve currencies such as the US dollar. Changes in central bank policies and gold reserve strategies can have a significant impact on gold prices and market dynamics.

RISE OF EMERGING MARKETS

Emerging economies, particularly in Asia, are becoming increasingly important players in the global gold market. Rising incomes, growing middle-class populations, and cultural affinity for gold as a store of value are driving demand for gold in these markets. As emerging economies continue to grow and develop, their demand for gold is expected to increase further, creating new opportunities for investors and traders. Additionally, emerging markets are playing an increasingly influential role in shaping the dynamics of the global gold market, influencing supply, demand, and price trends.

These emerging trends in the gold market are reshaping the way gold is traded, accessed, and perceived by investors. By understanding and embracing these trends, traders can position themselves to capitalize on new opportunities and navigate potential risks effectively in the evolving landscape of gold trading.

CHAPTER 33: TECHNOLOGICAL INNOVATIONS AND THEIR IMPACT

Technological innovations have been a game-changer in the gold trading industry, transforming how traders access, analyze, and execute trades. Here's an in-depth exploration of the impact of technological advancements on gold trading:

ELECTRONIC TRADING PLATFORMS:

The advent of electronic trading platforms has revolutionized gold trading by providing traders with seamless access to global markets. These platforms offer real-time market data, advanced charting tools, and lightning-fast trade execution capabilities.

Traders can access a wide range of gold products, including spot contracts, futures, options, and exchange-traded funds (ETFs), all from a single interface. Electronic trading platforms have democratized access to the gold market, allowing traders of all sizes to participate in gold trading with ease.

ARTIFICIAL INTELLIGENCE (AI) AND MACHINE LEARNING:

AI and machine learning technologies are increasingly being leveraged in gold trading for data analysis, pattern recognition, and predictive modeling. AI algorithms can analyze vast amounts of market data, identify trading patterns, and predict future price movements with a high degree of accuracy.

Machine learning algorithms can adapt and improve over time, continuously refining trading strategies based on evolving market conditions. AI-powered trading systems are capable of executing trades at lightning speed, capitalizing on market opportunities in real-time.

BLOCKCHAIN AND DISTRIBUTED LEDGER TECHNOLOGY (DLT):

Blockchain technology has the potential to revolutionize the gold market by improving transparency, security, and efficiency in trading and settlement processes. Blockchain-based platforms enable transparent tracking of gold transactions from mine to market, ensuring the authenticity and provenance of gold assets.

Smart contracts executed on blockchain networks facilitate secure and tamper-proof trade settlement, eliminating the need for intermediaries and reducing counterparty risk. Distributed ledger technology (DLT) has the potential to streamline gold trading processes, reduce transaction costs, and enhance market liquidity.

MOBILE TRADING APPS:

The rise of mobile trading apps has empowered traders to trade gold on the go, using their smartphones or tablets. Mobile trading apps offer intuitive interfaces, real-time market updates, and seamless trade execution capabilities, enabling traders to monitor and manage their portfolios from anywhere in the world. These apps cater to the needs of modern traders who value convenience and flexibility, allowing them to stay connected to the market and capitalize on opportunities at any time.

ROBO-ADVISORS AND AUTOMATED TRADING:

Robo-advisors and automated trading systems have gained popularity in the gold market, offering algorithmic-based investment advice and portfolio management services. These platforms use AI algorithms to analyze market trends, assess risk profiles, and construct diversified investment portfolios tailored to individual investor preferences.

Automated trading systems can execute trades automatically based on predefined rules and parameters, removing emotional biases and human errors from the trading process. Robo-advisors provide cost-effective solutions for investors seeking passive investment strategies and hands-off portfolio management.

These technological innovations have democratized access to the gold market, enhanced trading efficiency, and empowered traders with advanced tools and capabilities. Embracing technology is essential for staying competitive and maximizing opportunities in the ever-evolving landscape of gold trading. Traders who leverage technology effectively can gain a competitive edge and achieve greater success in the gold market.

PART 11: FINAL THOUGHTS

CHAPTER 34: FINAL TIPS FOR SUCCESSFUL GOLD TRADING

As you prepare to embark on your journey as a gold trader, armed with knowledge and insight into the intricacies of the market, it's essential to equip yourself with practical tips and strategies to navigate the dynamic landscape successfully. Here are some final tips to help you thrive in the world of gold trading:

CONTINUOUS LEARNING:

Stay Hungry for Knowledge: The gold market is vast and ever-changing. Keep yourself updated with the latest market developments, economic trends, and trading strategies through continuous learning. Attend seminars, read books, follow reputable financial news outlets, and engage with experienced traders to expand your knowledge base.

Learn from Experience: Experience is one of the most valuable teachers in trading. Reflect on your past trades, both successes and failures, and extract valuable lessons from them. Keep a trading journal to document your thoughts, decisions, and outcomes, and use it as a tool for self-improvement and growth.

DISCIPLINE AND PATIENCE:

Stick to Your Trading Plan: Develop a well-defined trading plan that outlines your objectives, risk tolerance, entry and exit criteria, and money management rules. Once established, adhere to your plan religiously, even in the face of temptation or uncertainty. Discipline is the cornerstone of successful trading.

Exercise Patience: Rome wasn't built in a day, and neither is a successful trading career. Be patient and realistic in your expectations. Understand that trading is a journey filled with ups and downs, and success often comes to those who persevere through the inevitable challenges.

RISK MANAGEMENT:

Protect Your Capital: Prioritize risk management above all else. Only risk a small percentage of your trading capital on any single trade, typically no more than 1-2% of your total account balance. Use stop-loss orders to limit potential losses and protect your capital from catastrophic drawdowns.

Focus on Risk-Reward: Before entering a trade, assess the potential risk-reward ratio to ensure that the potential reward justifies the risk taken. Aim for trades with favorable risk-reward profiles, where the potential reward outweighs the potential risk by a significant margin.

EMOTIONAL CONTROL:

Keep Your Emotions in Check: Emotions such as fear, greed, and overconfidence can cloud your judgment and lead to impulsive or irrational trading decisions. Practice emotional discipline by maintaining a calm and rational mindset, especially during times of market volatility or adversity.

Stick to Your Plan: Trust in your trading plan and stick to it, regardless of external market influences or emotional impulses. Avoid making spontaneous decisions based on fear or greed, and let your pre-established plan guide your actions.

ADAPTABILITY:

Be Flexible: The markets are dynamic and ever-changing, requiring traders to be flexible and adaptable in their approach.

Be willing to adjust your strategies and tactics based on shifting market conditions, new information, or unexpected events.

Embrace Change: Embrace change as an opportunity for growth and evolution. Stay open-minded and continuously seek ways to refine and improve your trading approach. Flexibility and adaptability are key traits of successful traders.

By incorporating these final tips into your trading arsenal, you'll be better equipped to navigate the challenges and opportunities of the gold market effectively. Remember that success in trading is not measured by the outcome of individual trades but by the consistency of your approach and your ability to learn and grow from every experience.

Keep striving for improvement, stay disciplined, and trust in your abilities as you embark on your journey towards becoming a successful gold trader.

CHAPTER 35: ENCOURAGEMENT FOR YOUR TRADING JOURNEY

Embarking on a trading journey is akin to setting sail on uncharted waters. It's an exhilarating adventure filled with excitement, challenges, and endless possibilities. As you navigate the vast and dynamic landscape of the gold market, it's important to keep a few key principles in mind to sustain you on your journey:

EMBRACE THE JOURNEY:

Understand that trading is a journey, not a destination. Embrace the process of learning, growing, and evolving as a trader. Each trade, whether a win or a loss, is an opportunity for growth and improvement. Approach your journey with curiosity, enthusiasm, and a willingness to learn from every experience.

CULTIVATE RESILIENCE:

Trading is not for the faint of heart. Setbacks and challenges are an inevitable part of the journey. Cultivate resilience by developing the mental fortitude to persevere through adversity. Learn from your mistakes, adapt to changing market conditions, and bounce back stronger with each setback.

STAY COMMITTED TO YOUR GOALS:

Define clear, achievable goals for your trading journey and stay committed to them. Whether your goal is to achieve consistent profitability, master a specific trading strategy, or build a sustainable trading career, maintain unwavering focus and dedication to your objectives.

SEEK CONTINUOUS IMPROVEMENT:

Trading is a skill that can be honed and refined over time. Commit yourself to a lifelong journey of continuous improvement. Invest in your education, seek out mentors and peers who can offer guidance and support, and actively seek feedback to identify areas for growth and development.

BUILD A SUPPORT SYSTEM:

Surround yourself with a supportive network of mentors, peers, and resources that can help you navigate the challenges of trading. Engage with trading communities, participate in forums and discussion groups, and seek out educational materials and resources to enhance your knowledge and skills.

MAINTAIN DISCIPLINE AND FOCUS:

Discipline is the bedrock of successful trading. Develop a disciplined approach to your trading, adhere to your trading plan with unwavering consistency, and maintain focus and composure, especially during times of market volatility or uncertainty.

CELEBRATE YOUR PROGRESS:

Celebrate your successes, no matter how small. Recognize and acknowledge the progress you've made on your trading journey, and use it as fuel to propel you forward. Take pride in your achievements and use them as motivation to continue striving for excellence.

STAY GROUNDED AND HUMBLE:

Remember that trading is humbling, and no trader is infallible. Stay grounded and humble in your approach, recognizing that there is always more to learn and room for improvement. Approach the markets with humility and respect, and never become complacent or overconfident.

As you set sail on your trading journey, remember that success is not defined by the outcome of individual trades but by the journey itself—the lessons learned, the skills acquired, and the personal growth experienced along the way. Embrace the challenges, celebrate the victories, and above all, enjoy the journey.

With dedication, perseverance, and a positive mindset, you have the power to achieve your trading goals and realize your full potential as a gold trader.

Wishing you all the best on your gold trading journey.

GLOSSARY OF GOLD TRADING TERMS

A

Ask Price: The price at which a seller is willing to sell an asset, such as gold.

Asset: Any item of value owned by an individual or corporation, including gold.

B

Bid Price: The price at which a buyer is willing to purchase an asset, such as gold.

Bull Market: A market condition where prices are rising or are expected to rise.

C

Call Option: A financial contract that gives the holder the right, but not the obligation, to buy an asset at a specified price within a specific period.

CFD (Contract for Difference): A derivative trading product that allows traders to speculate on price movements without owning the underlying asset.

Chart Pattern: A pattern formed by the price movements of an asset on a chart, used in technical analysis to predict future price movements.

Commodity: A basic good used in commerce that is interchangeable with other goods of the same type, such as gold.

D

Day Trading: The practice of buying and selling financial instruments within the same trading day.

Double Bottom: A bullish reversal pattern in technical analysis indicating a potential rise in price.

E

ETF (Exchange-Traded Fund): A marketable security that tracks an index, commodity, bonds, or a basket of assets, like an index fund, but trades like a stock.

Expiration Date: The date on which a derivative contract (options or futures) becomes void and the final settlement occurs.

F

Futures Contract: A standardized legal agreement to buy or sell an asset at a predetermined price at a specified time in the future.

G

Gold Standard: A monetary system where a country's currency or paper money has a value directly linked to gold.

H

Hedging: A strategy used to offset or reduce the risk of adverse price movements in an asset.

Head and Shoulders: A chart pattern in technical analysis indicating a trend reversal.

I

Intraday: Refers to the price movements of an asset within a single trading day.

L

Liquidity: The ease with which an asset can be converted into cash without affecting its market price.

M

MACD (Moving Average Convergence Divergence): A trend-following momentum indicator that shows the relationship between two moving averages of an asset's price.

Margin: The collateral that a trader must deposit to cover the credit risk of their trading activities.

O

Options Contract: A financial derivative that gives the buyer the right, but not the obligation, to buy or sell an asset at a specified price on or before a specified date.

Overbought: A condition where an asset is trading at a price higher than its intrinsic value, often indicated by technical analysis tools.

P

Put Option: A financial contract that gives the holder the right, but not the obligation, to sell an asset at a specified price within a specific period.

R

Resistance Level: A price level where selling pressure tends to prevent the price from rising further.

RSI (Relative Strength Index): A momentum oscillator that measures the speed and change of price movements.

S

Scalping: A trading strategy that involves making numerous trades to profit from small price movements.

Short Selling: The sale of an asset that the seller does not own, typically borrowed, with the intention of buying it back at a lower price.

Stop-Loss Order: An order placed to sell an asset when it reaches a certain price, used to limit potential losses.

Support Level: A price level where buying pressure tends to prevent the price from falling further.

T

Technical Analysis: The study of past market data, primarily price and volume, to forecast future price movements.

Trading Volume: The total number of shares or contracts traded for a particular asset during a specific time period.

V

Volatility: A statistical measure of the dispersion of returns for a given security or market index.

W

Whipsaw: A condition where a security's price heads in one direction, but then is followed quickly by a movement in the opposite direction.

This glossary covers essential terms used in gold trading, providing a foundational understanding for traders as they navigate the market.

RECOMMENDED READING AND RESOURCES

BOOKS

1. The New Case for Gold" by James Rickards

This book explores the importance of gold in modern finance and provides a compelling argument for including gold in your investment portfolio.

2. Guide to Investing in Gold & Silver" by Michael Maloney

A comprehensive guide to understanding the historical significance of precious metals and practical advice on investing in gold and silver.

3. Gold: The Once and Future Money" by Nathan Lewis

An in-depth exploration of gold's historical role in the global economy and its potential future.

4. Technical Analysis of the Financial Markets" by John J. Murphy

A must-read for traders, this book covers technical analysis comprehensively, including chart patterns, indicators, and trading systems.

5. The Little Book of Currency Trading" by Kathy Lien

A practical guide for traders at all levels, with strategies and tips specifically for currency trading, which includes gold trading pairs like XAU/USD.

WEBSITES

1. Kitco (www.kitco.com)

A leading source for gold news, market analysis, and real-time gold prices.

2. World Gold Council (www.gold.org)

Provides extensive information on gold supply and demand, research reports, and data on the gold market.

3. Investopedia (www.investopedia.com)

Offers a wide range of articles, tutorials, and resources on gold trading, technical analysis, and investing strategies.

4. TradingView (www.tradingview.com)

A social network for traders and investors on Stock, Futures, and Forex markets, offering advanced charting tools and a community of traders.

ONLINE COURSES

1. Coursera – "Financial Markets" by Yale University

This course provides a comprehensive overview of financial markets, including discussions on gold as an investment asset.

2. Udemy – "The Complete Foundation Stock Trading Course"

A foundational course that covers various trading strategies, technical analysis, and market fundamentals.

3. edX – "Introduction to Trading" by the University of Queensland

Offers an introduction to trading with a focus on financial markets, including gold.

BLOGS AND NEWSLETTERS

1. GoldSilver (www.goldsilver.com/blog)

A blog by Mike Maloney providing insights and analysis on the precious metals market.

2. BullionVault (www.bullionvault.com/gold-news)

Offers market news, analysis, and expert opinions on gold and silver trading.

3. DailyFX (www.dailyfx.com)

Provides daily market news, analysis, and insights on forex and commodities, including gold.

TOOLS AND SOFTWARE

1. MetaTrader 4 (MT4)

A popular trading platform for forex and commodities trading, offering advanced charting tools and automated trading capabilities.

2. ThinkorSwim by TD Ameritrade

A powerful trading platform with extensive tools for technical analysis and trading gold.

3. Bloomberg Terminal

Provides real-time data, news, and analytics for professional traders and investors.

COMMUNITY AND FORUMS

1. Elite Trader (www.elitetrader.com)

A forum for traders to discuss strategies, share insights, and learn from each other.

2. Forex Factory (www.forexfactory.com)

A popular forum for forex and commodities traders, offering discussions on market analysis, trading systems, and strategies.

3. Reddit – r/Gold

A subreddit dedicated to discussions on gold investing, market trends, and news.

Using these resources can greatly improve your comprehension of gold trading and equip you with the necessary tools and knowledge to excel in the market. Whether you're new to trading or a seasoned investor, these suggested readings and resources provide valuable insights and useful guidance.

SAMPLE TRADING PLAN TEMPLATES

Template 1: Basic Trading Plan

Section	Details
Trading Goals	Short-term Goal: 5% ROI per month
	Long-term Goal: 50% ROI within the first year
Trading Style	Day Trading: Short-term trades opened and closed within the same day
	Swing Trading: Positions held for several days
Market Analysis	Technical Analysis: Support/resistance levels, moving averages, MACD
	Fundamental Analysis: Economic indicators, geopolitical events, policies
Risk Management	Risk per Trade: 1-2% of trading capital
	Stop-Loss Orders: Set at 2% below entry price
	Take-Profit Orders: Set at 5% above entry price
Entry and Exit Rules	Entry Signals: Based on MACD crossovers, RSI levels, trendline breaks
	Exit Signals: Stop-loss or take-profit levels, technical indicator reversals
Trade Documentation	Trading journal logging date, entry/exit points, profit/loss, trade rationale
Review and Adjustments	Weekly and monthly performance reviews
	Adjust strategies based on performance and market conditions

Template 2: Intermediate Trading Plan

Section	Details
Trading Goals	Short-term Goal: $1,000 monthly income from trading
	Long-term Goal: $100,000 trading account within two years
Trading Style	Combination of Day Trading and Swing Trading
Market Analysis	Technical Analysis: Candlestick patterns, Fibonacci retracements, volume analysis
	Fundamental Analysis: Economic data releases, gold mining reports, inflation rates
Risk Management	Risk per Trade: 1% of total capital
	Portfolio Diversification: Allocate funds across ETFs, futures, currency pairs
	Stop-Loss Orders: 1.5% below entry price
	Take-Profit Orders: 3% above entry price
Entry and Exit Rules	Entry Signals: Confirm trades with two technical indicators (e.g., RSI and Bollinger Bands)
	Exit Signals: Stop-loss or take-profit levels, changing market conditions
Trade Documentation	Detailed trade records with chart screenshots and notes on trade rationale
Review and Adjustments	Weekly trade reviews
	Monthly performance analysis
	Regular updates to the trading plan based on insights and market developments

Template 3: Advanced Trading Plan

Section	Details
Trading Goals	Short-term Goal: 8% monthly ROI
	Long-term Goal: $500,000 trading capital within five years
Trading Style	Combination of Scalping, Day Trading, and Position Trading
Market Analysis	Technical Analysis: Elliott Wave Theory, Ichimoku Cloud, advanced chart patterns
	Fundamental Analysis: Macroeconomic trends, central bank policies, major geopolitical events
Risk Management	Risk per Trade: 0.5-1% of total capital
	Advanced Hedging: Use options and futures for hedging major positions
	Stop-Loss Orders: Dynamic based on volatility
	Take-Profit Orders: Trailing take-profit orders for maximizing gains
Entry and Exit Rules	Entry Signals: Advanced confirmation from multiple indicators and pattern alignments
	Exit Signals: Trailing stops, pivot points, major support/resistance breakouts
Trade Documentation	Comprehensive trading journal with detailed logs, emotional state notes, periodic performance reviews
Review and Adjustments	Daily, weekly, and monthly reviews
	Continuous learning and strategy refinement based on performance data and market research

ABOUT THE AUTHOR

Usiere Uko

Usiere Uko is a Consultant, ILO Certified Trainer, and Business & Finance Author focused on financial independence and entrepreneurship. A former oil and gas engineer turned entrepreneur, he helps individuals and business owners build sustainable income, make smarter financial decisions, and grow resilient businesses.

He is a certified Business Development Service Provider (BDSP) and an ILO-certified trainer in SIYB and WIDB, and currently serves as Lead Consultant at Sageway Consulting and Training Coordinator at The Citadel Business Academy.

Usiere writes in a friendly and practical style, making complex financial and business ideas simple, clear, and actionable for everyday readers and entrepreneurs. He is based in Lagos, Nigeria.

BOOKS IN THIS SERIES
COMMODITIES TRADING FOR BEGINNERS

Gold Trading 101: The Beginner's Guide To Unlocking The Potential Of Precious Metals

Silver Trading 101: Smart Strategies For Silver Trading Beginners

Oil Trading 101: Understanding The Basics Of Trading The Oil Market, Cfds, Futures And Options

Natural Gas Trading 101: A Beginner's Guide To Profiting From The Energy Market

BOOKS BY THIS AUTHOR

Practical Steps To Financial Freedom And Independence: Money Management Skills For Beginners

Before You Trade Forex: Things You Need To Know If You Desire To Start Trading Forex Profitably

Before You Invest In Cryptocurrency: A Simple Guide To Understanding The Cryptocurrency Market

101 Common Money Mistakes To Avoid: And How To Fix Them. Book 1: Expenses. Money Management, Making Your Budget Work

How To Avoid Living Under Financial Pressure: A Simple Guide To Getting Back Control Of Your Finances

Financial Independence For Employees: Making

Your Job A Stepping Stone To Exiting The Rat Race And Living Your Dreams

Managing Your Money Post Covid: Financial Management Skills For An Era Of High Inflation And Market Disruption

Retire On Your Own Terms: A Simple Guide To Financially Literate Retirement Planning

Your Ultimate Money Makeover: Manage Your Money Better, Take Control Of Your Finances And Your Life

Teaching Kids Money 101: Simple Parenting Strategies For Raising Financially Literate Kids From Toddler To Teen Years And Beyond

Uncle Ben's Money Lessons: Book I: Do You Want To Work For Money? A Vacation Story With An Adventure Into The World Of Money

Nft Investing 101: A Beginner's Guide To Collectible Digital Assets

Stock Market Investing 101: A Practical Beginners

Guide To Online And Offline Stock Trading

Investing In Etfs 101: A Beginner's Guide For Building Wealth With Exchange-Traded Funds

Day Trading 101: A Complete Beginner's Guide To Trading The Markets

Forex Trading 101: A Beginner's Guide And Strategies To Profitable Currency Trading

Options Trading 101: A Beginner's Guide To Trading Stock Options

Futures Trading 101: A Step-By-Step Guide And Strategies For Beginner Traders

www.ingramcontent.com/pod-product-compliance
Lightning Source LLC
Chambersburg PA
CBHW071453220526
45472CB00003B/782